I enthusiastically recommend *Activating Mira*... an international evangelist who has seen the miraculous on a ... g basis. The content will equip believers to step into a life of supernatural faith without reservation. The goal is to inspire the next generation to view the supernatural as something natural for Christ followers. Enjoy the read and watch your faith grow.

—*Doug Clay*
General Superintendent of the Assemblies of God
Springfield, MO

There are lots of books on the market about faith; however, this one by Chris Mikkelson brings an entirely different perspective to the daily Christian life and what we might be missing. With personal stories that inspire as well as draw us in, he shares how God has moved in ways unexpected by most Christians today; yet Chris expects them, and God moves in miraculous ways! He shares how total belief in God's Word and reliance on the Holy Spirit will transform not only your life in general but also your daily walk with the Lord. This book will inspire you to step into a world that flows with the power of God and brings not only healing, restoration, and joy but also salvation and miracles. Enjoy the read and be prepared to move into a higher level of life with the supernatural power of God.

—*Pastor Larry Huch*
Founding pastor, DFW New Beginnings Church
Bedford, TX

Activating Miracles is a compelling and inspiring guide to unlocking the power of supernatural faith within every believer. Chris's personal stories of miraculous encounters and his unwavering belief in the truth of God's Word make this book a captivating read. Through his insights and encouragement, Chris empowers readers to embrace the miraculous in their everyday lives, touching the world around them with healing and deliverance. A true testament to the transformative power of faith, this book will ignite a flame of hope and inspire readers to step boldly into the realm of the supernatural. Prepare to be activated!

—*Nathan Morris*
Founder and President, Shake The Nations Ministries
Apopka, FL

My spirit is so stirred for this powerful new book, *Activating Miracles*, by my friend Evangelist Chris Mikkelson. This book will stir your heart to live in the realm of seeing the impossible happen. It will not only awaken your faith but also guide you into a life of miracles. Chris has traveled the world sharing the gospel. His message is one that calls all within earshot to experience the love and freedom of Christ! If you are ready to experience next-level faith and defeat obstacles from the enemy, read this book!

—*Pat Schatzline*
Evangelist, author, and CEO, Remnant Ministries International
Fort Worth, TX

It was in 2014 that I first had the chance to meet and interface with Chris Mikkelson. He was taking point in preparation for a Reinhard Bonnke crusade at the BBVA soccer stadium in Houston, Texas, that was scheduled for February 2015. We gave Chris and his team the use of some of our ministry offices in Houston, as they needed to spend a few months preparing for the event. Immediately, I was intrigued by his life story, his level of commitment and faith, his character, as well as his genuine passion for God and people.

You will find his book, *Activating Miracles*, quite engaging and spiritually provoking. His personal story, life message, and real-life encounters will stir your faith and vision. Many speak and write from theory, yet Chris uniquely combines his experiences with his gift of communication and teaching, to spotlight what the Lord is doing in and through those who yield themselves to His purposes and calling in their lives. This book is filled with teaching, Scripture, the leading and power of the Holy Spirit, as well as the supernatural touch of God upon a life available to Him.

Time, consistency, and fruitfulness of life and ministry have proven to me the depth and breadth of the passion and calling in Chris and Amanda Mikkelson's lives. Take the time to draw from their spiritual well and journey in the pages of this book. You'll be blessed that you did.

—*Doug Stringer*
Founder and president, Somebody Cares America; Somebody Cares International; and Turning Point Ministries, International
Houston, TX

I have had the honor of getting to know Chris Mikkelson through the GEA (Global Evangelists Alliance), and he is a man who is devoted to knowing Jesus and spreading the power of the gospel throughout the nations. Chris is an evangelist whom God is raising up in this last hour to sound the call for the power of the gospel throughout the nation. In his book, *Activating Miracles*, Chris creates a simple road map for the reader to follow, which is the footsteps of Jesus. Faith in Jesus spells TRUST. Trusting the Word of God over feelings is what Chris wonderfully lays out in this book. I pray God blesses you as you read this resource and that it will inspire faith that points you to Jesus and the power of God's Word.

—*Chris Overstreet*
Author and evangelist, Compassion to Action
Vancouver, WA

The prophet Isaiah declared the Word of the Lord for the day we are living in: *"Arise, shine; for your light has come! And the glory of the LORD is risen upon you. For behold, the darkness shall cover the earth, And deep darkness the people; but the LORD will arise over you, and His glory will be seen upon you"* (Isaiah 60:1–2). Chris Mikkelson has proclaimed the kingdom of God in some of the darkest places on the planet and seen powerful breakthroughs. Read his book—you will be greatly encouraged to shine no matter how dark your environment is.

—*Tom Crandall*
Senior Leadership Team, Bethel Church
Redding, CA
Founder and overseer of evangelism, 1hope4America

I know few people who have displayed such demonstrative power amidst massive open-air evangelistic meetings and walk in humility and kindness as Chris Mikkelson. These pages contain the heart and wisdom of the man. I encourage each person who feels called to preach the gospel with signs and wonders following to open these pages and learn what has been so deeply revealed to Chris over years of walking with God in the fields of harvest.

—*Eric Gilmour*
Author/speaker, Sonship International

Activating Miracles by Chris Mikkelson will call you higher into your faith walk. It teaches you what faith is and how to grow and cultivate the God-given faith within you. Each chapter will challenge you as well as uplift you.

—*Mikel French*
Evangelist, Mikel French Ministries
Tulsa, OK

Chris and Amanda Mikkelson have brought the Good News of the gospel to millions, face-to-face, in limited-access regions. Their proven, anointed ministry is marked by supernatural miracles wherever they go. *Activating Miracles* is your handbook for going deeper into the mission and power of Jesus. Get ready for your activation!

—*Tim Enloe*
Evangelist/teacher, EnloeMinistries.org

Chris Mikkelson's book, *Activating Miracles*, will cause your faith to skyrocket to new, incredible levels. His stories will inspire you, and his teaching will equip you to really understand how faith works. There is a new dimension of God's power awaiting you as you read the pages of this book. You will be empowered to see God's healing and deliverance flow in people's lives. You will be activated in authentic faith without limits. I loved reading this book and personally learned so much from it!

—*Matt Sorger*
Prophetic minister; health transformation coach; author, *God's Unstoppable Breakthrough*; host, *Unstoppable God* television show

CHRIS MIKKELSON

ACTIVATING
MIRACLES

ENTER INTO
SUPERNATURAL FAITH
WITHOUT LIMITS

WHITAKER
HOUSE

ACTIVATING MIRACLES:
Enter into Supernatural Faith Without Limits

Chris Mikkelson
1711 Amazing Way, Ste. 216
Ocoee, FL 34761
www.chrismikkelson.com

ISBN: 979-8-88769-100-8
eBook ISBN: 979-8-88769-101-5
Printed in the United States of America
© 2024 by Chris Mikkelson

Whitaker House
1030 Hunt Valley Circle
New Kensington, PA 15068
www.whitakerhouse.com

Library of Congress Control Number: 2023950786

1 2 3 4 5 6 7 8 9 10 11 **UJ** 31 30 29 28 27 26 25 24

DEDICATION

I dedicate this book to my beautiful wife, Amanda, who has been by my side since we met in 2005 and received Jesus together in 2006. Amanda, you are the greatest gift God has ever given to me. You are my best friend, my greatest ally, my biggest supporter and fan. You have been with me through all the highs and lows of life and ministry, and you have stood by me faithfully every step of the way. I love you more today than ever before, and I couldn't do any of this without you by my side. You encouraged me so many times to write this book, even when I wanted to give up, and you have always believed in me. I love you dearly—now and forever.

I also dedicate this book to all those who have stood with us at Chris Mikkelson Evangelistic Ministries as prayer partners and financial supporters. You make it possible for us to see millions of souls saved around the world in the most unreached places on the planet, and for that, I am eternally grateful.

CONTENTS

FOREWORD

The late nineteenth century into the early twentieth century was a time of palpable tension between science and religion. Debates raged not only in the religious world but in secular academia, as well. The rise of scientific inquiry and skepticism during this period led to a growing need for theologians to address the compatibility of miracles with a rapidly evolving naturalistic worldview. One landmark book, *Counterfeit Miracles*, by theologian Benjamin Breckinridge Warfield (published in 1918), captured the zeitgeist of scholarship in this era. In his book, Warfield embraced biblical miracles but argued that all supposed modern "miracles" are fraudulent hoaxes that should be treated with the utmost suspicion.

While Warfield's book was pivotal, his ideas were not wholly original. Warfield was heavily influenced by his predecessor, Conyers Middleton, who wrote on the same subject a hundred years earlier.

Middleton's work explored the notion of miracles within the framework of natural laws, suggesting that natural causes could explain phenomena once attributed to divine intervention. Middleton was a famous historian and theologian. He was also a rationalist, heavily influenced by Enlightenment thinkers. His philosophy was more deist than Christian, and his work, *Free Inquiry*, was a polemic aimed at supernatural claims, miraculous signs, and mysticism, particularly of the Catholic Church. His stated aim was to distance Protestantism from Catholic superstition. His method was to prove that all miracles ceased within the first century and to discredit modern miracle claims. Yet one cannot help but notice that Middleton's skepticism seemed to go beyond merely the suspicious modern miraculous claims. "The history of the Gospel, I hope, may be true," he said, "though the history of the Church be fabulous."

Interestingly, none other than John Wesley himself took Middleton to task in a letter of response with blistering language and harsh criticism. He accused Middleton of contradicting himself, having lost his way, being dishonest, and secretly aiming his polemic against "the fanatics who wrote the Bible." In other words, if the same skepticism being applied to modern miracle claims were applied to Scripture itself, to be consistent, Middleton would have to reject the biblical stories as well. What Wesley powerfully argued, and what I believe is indisputable from Scripture, is that there is no consistently rational reason for anyone who believes the Bible is true to doubt the possibility of miracles today.

Thankfully, in our time, the ideas of Middleton and Warfield have been rejected by most of the church around the world. There is now little doubt among most Christians that God still can and does do miracles. In fact, some of our most brilliant scholars and philosophers powerfully argue in favor of a supernatural (one might say, miraculous) worldview. Their compelling theological arguments are reinforced by an unabating deluge of reports of miracles happening all over the world. It's a good time for Christian believers!

And yet many of us have been infected by a more subtle kind of cessationism—a kind of doubt that has not been formalized in our theology; in fact, it runs counter to it. We might say that we believe in miracles, but deep down, we wonder. Perhaps it's easier to accept the miracles of the Bible because they are far away from us in space and time. Believing in them demands nothing of us at this moment. What is much more difficult to believe is that a miracle can happen right here, right now, to me. This kind of unbelief creates its own kind of cognitive dissonance. It also creates believing unbelievers. While it may reject the overt cynicism of critics like Warfield and Middleton, the outcome is the same: practical cessationism.

One reason for this difficulty is that many have never seen a miracle in person, even if they believe miracles occur. Moreover, many wouldn't recognize a miracle, even if they did see one. This is because, often, when people think of the word *miracle*, they imagine something from a fantasy movie or Disney cartoon. Some people think of miracles as synonymous with magic and nonsense. But what if *miracle* is just another word for what God does every day through the lives of ordinary believers? What if miracles are not just events reserved for biblical times or distant lands but are invitations for each of us to participate actively in the divine tapestry of faith and wonder? That is precisely what Chris Mikkelson, a global evangelist with a heart ablaze for the gospel, presents in *Activating Miracles: Enter into Supernatural Faith Without Limits*.

In a world that often feels dominated by fear and doubt, Chris emerges as a voice that speaks from the frontlines of faith. He has stood before large crowds in regions where Christianity struggles to maintain a foothold, daring to declare the gospel in places many might deem impossible. With a ministry rooted in real-world action, Chris doesn't merely talk about faith—he embodies it.

I hired Chris as an assistant when he was a young man fresh out of Bible school. He was full of enthusiasm and optimism. He traveled the world with me, saw the miraculous with his own eyes, and then left to start his evangelistic ministry from scratch. Having witnessed Chris' journey over many years, I can attest that his transformation from a faithful servant to a fearless carrier of God's Word is a testament to the principles he shares within these pages.

Activating Miracles is not a book of theoretical musings; it's a road map penned by a practitioner. Chris brings to life a faith journey that begins and ends with Jesus. Each chapter uncovers the layers of faith that are not confined to moments of ecstatic spiritual highs but anchored in everyday encounters with Christ. He reminds us that faith is not a magic formula but a journey of trust that transcends circumstances, erases fear, and redefines perspective. As you traverse these chapters, you'll immerse yourself in the heart of faith's DNA. Chris dismantles the barriers we often erect between the natural and supernatural, revealing that miracles are not just historical relics but actual events as accessible as the air we breathe. He navigates themes of trust, the battle against fear, overcoming adversity, and ultimately expanding the kingdom of God throughout the earth.

What sets *Activating Miracles* apart is Chris' authenticity. His voice resonates with the joy of a child who has discovered an unending treasure, and his words are seasoned with the wisdom of one who has experienced the reality of God's miraculous touch. The playful tone that infuses these pages reminds us that faith is a journey of joyful exploration, where we are invited to dance with the divine in the most unexpected ways. So, as you embark on this journey through *Activating Miracles*, prepare to have your faith stirred, your expectations expanded, and your doubts dismantled. May these pages ignite the spark of supernatural faith within you and lead you into a realm where limitations are shattered, and authentic miracles are activated—not just in theory but in your life, today!

With joyful anticipation,
Daniel Kolenda
President and CEO, Christ for All Nations
Lead Pastor, Nations Church
Orlando, FL

PREFACE

God has an amazing plan for you, where He will use you to do great and mighty things. I believe God is bringing forth a new generation of people like you who will trust completely in His holy Word and confront their fears and the enemy of their souls with faith and power. If you're reading this book, you are part of that generation of faith-filled believers God wants to use to reach out with boldness and miraculous power.

However, a war rages to stop you and all other believers from doing this very thing. It's a war on faith—not a physical war fought with people and weapons but a spiritual war against our faith, against what we believe about Jesus Christ. We live in a day and time when our faith is being tried on every side. When you turn on the news, all you hear is fear. Nearly every commercial, TV show, and newscast perpetuates fear. Fear of death, fear of losing, fear of failure, fear of sickness, and fear of impossible circumstances. Every show makes us wonder what will happen next. "How are they going to get through this one?" we think. "They'll never make it. Maybe I'll never make it, either. It's too impossible."

These broadcasts are causing Christians of every denomination to start believing the fear-based media narrative rather than the Word of God. It is the plan of the enemy for Christians to believe that they aren't going to do great things, that they are living without hope and purpose in life. Convincing us we're not going to make it is Satan's primary plan.

This is where faith comes in. I believe we're living in a time in history when we need to take back the ground we've given up to the enemy and inspire a new generation of faith-filled believers to live radical lives for Jesus Christ. To inspire them to believe in God, no matter how hard things get, standing up with faith and power, and trusting in God for great things once again. When it appears to be our darkest hour, this is our time to shine the brightest, for the light always shines brightest when it's the darkest. It is your time to shine, and the key to shining bright for Jesus is *faith*!

We serve a miracle-working God who created the world with a single word. Rabbi Abraham Joshua Heschel, who marched with Dr. Martin Luther King, Jr., was known to say, "Words create worlds."[1] God created a world where deaf ears are opened, blind eyes see, and the paralyzed walk again. The God who can save the sinner's soul can also raise the dead! But how do we start moving in this kind of miraculous power? With faith!

Over the last decade, I have traveled around the world preaching the gospel of Jesus Christ in some of the most remote, difficult, dangerous places on the planet. I have faced darkness and difficulties head-on, and I have seen Jesus show up and multitudes of people be swept into the kingdom of God as a result. We have seen countless miracles of healing, signs, and wonders. The blind see, the crippled walk, the deaf hear, and the gospel is preached to millions in the face of many challenges. You,

---

1. Evangelical Lutheran Church in America, *AMMPARO* (Accompanying Migrants with Protection, Advocacy, Representation and Opportunities), "Words Create Worlds," https://download.elca.org/ELCA%20Resource%20Repository/AMMPARO_Words_Create_Worlds.pdf.

too, will see the glory of God. We were made for miracles, and this book will activate you into the miraculous like never before, in Jesus's name.

In this book, you will discover keys to entering into supernatural faith so that you can activate the miraculous in your life. Faith that will overcome fear, anxiety, depression, sickness, financial distress, family issues, and every other obstacle that might come your way. I believe this book will empower you to start moving in miraculous power. You will step into a realm of the impossible and see miracles of healing, signs, wonders, supernatural provision, and souls being saved like never before. Get ready to activate miracles through supernatural faith without limits, in Jesus's name!

ONE

ALL THINGS ARE POSSIBLE

"Faith does not operate in the realm of the possible. There is no glory for God in that which is humanly possible. Faith begins where man's power ends."
—*George Mueller*

"Jesus said to him, '[You say to Me,] "If You can?" All things are possible for the one who believes and trusts [in Me]!'"
—Mark 9:23 (AMP)

God has given me a burning desire to bring the gospel to the darkest, most unreached places on the earth. One of those places is Peshawar, Pakistan, a city located on the Afghanistan border in the northern mountain region. It was the headquarters of Al-Qaeda before 9/11 and is still a difficult area in that part of the world. Peshawar is one of the most dangerous cities in Pakistan to share the Gospel of Jesus Christ. Even the Christian pastors within the country don't want to go there to preach! But Peshawar was at the top of my list!

Six years earlier, God spoke to me, "I want you to put your other international crusades on hold and concentrate on the country of Pakistan for the time being. I want you to bring My gospel message to the people throughout that region of the world." Pakistan was not high on my original list of countries for ministry to be perfectly honest. It is very dangerous, especially for Christians. Yet, the Lord's voice was clear, and I wanted to obey Him.

For the last six years, we have traveled throughout Pakistan, holding open-air crusades in small and large towns, in villages and cities, seeing nearly two million people come to salvation in Jesus Christ! We don't call them "crusades" in Pakistan, as the word *crusade* has a negative connotation for Muslims. Rather, we call them "Good News Festivals" or "Gospel Festivals." Most Christians around the world know the term *crusade* because evangelist Billy Graham and many others have made the term famous. It has been a truly blessed time, and my love for the country and the Pakastani people has grown.

Still, my desire to go to Peshawar remained unchanged through those years. Then, in the spring of 2023, the Lord spoke to our team, "Now is the time!" We were so excited to experience what God was about to do. That fall, we made our twenty-third trip to Pakistan.

GOD HAS GIVEN ME A BURNING DESIRE TO BRING THE GOSPEL TO THE DARKEST, MOST UNREACHED PLACES ON THE EARTH.

A FLOW OF THE HOLY SPIRIT

On our way to Peshawar, we drove near the area where Osama bin Laden's hideout had been located by the US Navy SEALs Team 6. I'm always curious and wanted to get a closer look, but our local contact was quick to tell me it was *off limits*! As we drove into the city of Peshawar, you could feel the *spiritual* darkness, and you could see the *physical* darkness of the region—in the buildings, in the people's clothing—none of it was what we experience in the rest of Pakistan. We met a few Christian pastors for prayer at a church and then headed to the open-air field for the crusade. I knew it wasn't going to be a large crowd, but that was okay. We were finally in the city of Peshawar, and I just wanted to share the gospel of Jesus Christ to anyone who came.

We were shocked by what greeted us when we finally walked onstage. Over 35,000 people were gathered in that field in the city of Peshawar to the hear the message of salvation in Jesus! As soon as I opened my mouth to preach, the Holy Spirit started moving in power. I don't believe I have ever preached the gospel more clearly to the people in that region of the world before that night. There was such a flow of the Holy Spirit throughout the whole message. I was overwhelmed with God's presence. I knew it wasn't me. I knew that it was God who was giving me the words, God who was speaking through me by His Holy Spirit. I had become just a vessel for Him. How many of us want to pray, "Lord, I just want to be a vessel for You, a conduit that You can just flow through to reach the world around me"? It is a tremendous blessing to be used as a vessel of the Holy Spirit!

You could almost hear a pin drop as I unashamedly preached the good news of Jesus Christ as the only One who can save us from our sins. When I made the altar call for salvation, more than 24,000 people stood up and received Jesus Christ as their Lord and Savior for the very first time! Thousands were swept into the kingdom of God that night, and that is what it is all about. It was glorious!

After I made the call for salvation, I prayed for the sick; and, just as it says in Mark 16:20, God confirmed the Word through accompanying signs. Many came forward and testified that they had been healed that night during the prayer time. The greatest miracle of all is why we went there—and why we will continue to evangelize in the name of Jesus: the miracle of salvation. Praise God! Now, the follow-up process will be in full swing as the local pastors and leaders begin reaching out to these new believers so that they may join area churches for discipleship.

Some people ask me how Pakistan is even open to Christian crusades. Amazingly, their nation's constitution allows for freedom of expression for all religions. However, there are still many challenges that we face with radical groups in the area. Less than 2 percent of the population are Christians, but there are thousands of pastors and churches throughout Pakistan who are on fire for the gospel of Jesus Christ.

In numbers, this wasn't a big crusade for us since we often have much bigger crowds in other parts of Pakistan. However, I believe that in the spiritual world it was the biggest crusade I ever had the honor to preach. It was the fulfilling of Joel's prophecy, *"And it shall come to pass afterward that I will pour out My Spirit on all flesh"* (Joel 2:28). Hallelujah! The Lord is pouring out His Holy Spirit today! And He doesn't want to just pour out His Spirit on big crusades and in big churches; He wants to pour out His Spirit on the street corners, in the grocery stores, in the Walmart in your town and in mine! The harvest is plentiful—there are millions of people who are open and ready for the gospel. You can't reap it until you preach it! Will you do your part to spread the gospel and expand the kingdom of God in Jesus's name?

THE GREATEST MIRACLE OF ALL IS WHY WE
WENT THERE—AND WHY WE WILL CONTINUE
TO EVANGELIZE IN THE NAME OF JESUS:
THE MIRACLE OF SALVATION.

GOD WASN'T FINISHED WITH THE STORY

Two weeks after I returned from Peshawar, my wife, Amanda, and I were selling some furniture online. A man drove up to the house to pick up his purchase, and I met him in our front yard. We started talking, and he said, "Before I go overseas, I want to take care of this for my wife." I discovered that he was a former Navy SEAL and now was working as an overseas contractor. What came tumbling out of his mouth next amazed me. Before his retirement, this man was a part of the Navy SEALs—specifically, SEAL Team 6—and had made many trips into Pakistan. Surprised, I told him, "I was just there! I have just returned from Peshawar!" He had obviously spent a considerable amount of time there. We were both amazed at the "coincidence." In fact, he shared some information about his time as a SEAL Team 6 member that I can't share in this book, but we both knew this wasn't a coincidence; God had orchestrated this meeting.

With the ice broken between us, this retired Navy SEAL began to pour out his heart to me. The military life he lived was extremely stressful, and it took its toll on him; he felt broken and without hope. Years before, he had turned away from the church and believed he had nowhere to go for help. Silently, I was calling out to God, "Lord! What should I do? What should I say that will minister to this devastated man? I know he needs You, Jesus." Then I asked the man, "Can I tell you about Jesus?" He answered yes, and I began to share the gospel with him. He had heard much of it years earlier or from Navy chaplains, but now I shared how Jesus would completely transform his life. "If you just turn to Jesus today, He'll save you, He'll forgive you, He'll wash all your sins away. Do you want Jesus to forgive you and save you today?" I asked him.

That day, on my front lawn, this Navy SEAL Team 6 retiree said yes to Jesus, and he was born again in Jesus's name! My Bible says that all of heaven rejoices when one person comes to the Lord, the same way heaven rejoices when all those people accepted Jesus in Peshawar. I hope to meet up with this man again when he returns from his overseas job assignment. Just remember, God is looking for people like you and me who will say, "Jesus, use me, fill me, help me turn my world upside down for You!"

My friends, God's plan for each of our lives is a plan of supernatural encounters like this. We serve the God of the impossible. He knows our very thoughts, and He can orchestrate supernatural events like this in our lives. As we continue through this book, you will find that God is a supernatural God who loves to do the miraculous through ordinary people like you and me. God will take any ordinary person and make them extraordinary by the power of His Spirit, and you will see the miraculous in Jesus's name!

ALL THINGS ARE POSSIBLE FOR THE ONE WHO BELIEVES

All things are possible for the one who believes. A powerful lesson on faith for the impossible comes from the story of a father whose son desperately needed a miracle. It began as Jesus walked down from the mountain with Peter, James, and John after His transfiguration. A crowd of people and scribes were arguing with the rest of His disciples. When the crowd saw Jesus, they rushed over to Him. What followed is an incredible passage from Mark, chapter nine, on the power of faith.

One man from the crowd stepped toward Jesus, saying, *"Teacher, I brought You my son, who has a mute spirit. And wherever it seizes him, it throws him down; he foams at the mouth, gnashes his teeth, and becomes rigid. So I spoke to Your disciples, that they should cast it out, but they could not."* (Mark 9:17–18). Jesus's answer was a rebuke to His disciples: *"O faithless generation, how long shall I be with you? How long shall I bear with you? Bring him to Me"* (verse 19). So the father brought his son to Jesus. And as soon as the boy saw Jesus, *"immediately the spirit convulsed him, and he fell on the ground and wallowed, foaming at the mouth"* (verse 20). Jesus asked the father, *"How long has this been happening to him?"* (verse 21). The father sadly replied, *"From childhood. And often he has thrown him both into the fire and into the water to destroy him"* (verses 21–22). Then the father gave an impassioned plea: *"But **if You can do anything**, have compassion on us and help us"* (verse 22). *"Jesus said to him, 'If you can believe, all things are possible to him who believes'"* (verse 23).

Let's take another look at Mark 9:23, this time in the *Amplified* version: *"Jesus said to him, '[You say to Me,]* **"If You can?"** *All things are possible for the one who believes and trusts [in Me]!'"* (Mark 9:23 AMP). All things are possible to the one who *believes and trusts in Jesus*. At first, the boy's father wasn't sure if Jesus could help him. He didn't know, so he asked, in effect, "If You can do anything, then please have compassion on us and help us." In many Bible versions, Jesus's response is translated as a question: *"If you can?"* It's as though Jesus was saying to this man, "If you can? You mean *if I can? Of course, I can!* I'm Jesus. Have faith! Believe! All things are possible to the one who believes and trusts in Me." Immediately, the father realized who he was talking to, and he cried out, *"Lord, I believe; help my unbelief!"* (Mark 9:24).

You see, right there is the key. The father recognized who Jesus was when He cried out with tears, calling Him, "Lord!" I love that. Responding in that way meant that he submitted himself to Jesus. It's as though the father said, "Wait a minute. This isn't just some regular person. This is Jesus! Jesus, You are Lord. I submit my life to You, Lord. I believe." Then, he was honest enough to add, "...*help my unbelief!*" At that moment, Jesus performed the miracle, and the boy was completely healed and set free. That is the power of Jesus. (See Mark 9:25.)

"IF I CAN? OF COURSE, I CAN! I'M JESUS. HAVE FAITH! BELIEVE!"

FAITH FOR THE IMPOSSIBLE

My friends, faith for the impossible is not just about intellectual belief. It's not just saying, "Yes, I believe in God." No, all things are possible to the one who believes *and trusts in Jesus*. It's about Jesus. It's all about Jesus. We must get back to putting our faith in Him. It's not about anything else. It's not about you; it's not about me. It's all about Jesus. *"If you can believe, all things are possible to the one who believes* [and trusts in Jesus]" (Mark 9:23). The word *believe* in this verse is the Greek word *pisteuó*. It literally means to have faith that is a credit or to have confidence in something. By implication, it means to *entrust yourself* to something or someone, to believe, to commit to.[2] When you believe for the impossible, it's not just mind over matter. You must entrust yourself to the One who can do it, because you and I cannot do anything without Jesus.

---

2. Strong's Greek: 4100. πιστεύω (pisteuó) — to believe, entrust (biblehub.com).

When you're in a difficult situation, and you don't know how to get out of it, believe upon Jesus. Put your faith and trust in Him, and He will make a way where there seems to be no way. Maybe you're the only one who believes for the answer to an obstacle in your life. Maybe you're the only one in your Christian circle who believes. Maybe you're the only Christian in your family. You can still stand on the Word of God, because all things are possible to the one who believes and trusts in Jesus.

I've seen it happen so many times—the Holy Spirit moves in answer to faith, and God does the impossible. He shows up and people are healed, people are touched, people are delivered, people are set free, when we choose to take a position of faith. "If you can?" Jesus asked that father. Of course, He can! He is the King of kings and Lord of lords, God in the flesh! There have been crusades that we shouldn't have been able to conduct in the natural, but they became possible because we took a position of faith, and the Holy Spirit responded.

When you step out and begin to do something by faith in God, He will do the impossible through you. That's how it works. God is waiting for us. He says, "You heal the sick; you cast out demons." It's not our power doing it; it's God's power alone! But it's not going to happen unless you step out and begin to believe God. Nothing will happen unless you do something. Faith is an action. It can't be faith unless there's some kind of corresponding action. That word "believe" literally means to *entrust yourself* to somebody else. So, entrust yourself to Jesus.

YOU MUST ENTRUST YOURSELF TO THE ONE WHO CAN DO IT, BECAUSE YOU AND I CANNOT DO ANYTHING WITHOUT JESUS.

SEE THE INVISIBLE, EXPECT THE IMPOSSIBLE

"Faith sees the invisible, believes the unbelievable, and receives the impossible." These are dynamic words from Corrie ten Boom.

See the invisible, expect the impossible—Jesus lived in a constant state of expecting the impossible. Five loaves and two fish could feed 5,000 people in His world, all because the input of His life was not limited by His circumstances. Jesus viewed every situation through the eyes of His Father and could expect the impossible. Isaiah prophesied concerning Jesus, *"He will not judge by what he sees with his eyes, or decide by what he hears with his ears"* (Isaiah 11:3 NIV). Jesus would follow the voice of His Father alone. The source of input in His life was beyond this world, *"For I have not spoken on My own authority; but the Father who sent Me gave Me a command, what I should say and what I should speak. And I know that His command is everlasting life. Therefore, whatever I speak, just as the Father has told Me, so I speak"* (John 12:49–50). Jesus didn't speak from His own initiative but from the Father's eternal perspective. We need to see from God's eternal perspective as well.

Paul also reminds us that we cannot do the impossible until we see the invisible, which comes from God. *"We do not look at the things which are seen, but at the things which are not seen. For the things which are seen are temporary, but the things which are not seen are eternal"* (2 Corinthians 4:18). Jesus taught the disciples a lesson on having faith to do the impossible with the story of the withered fig tree.

As the disciples walked together, they saw a withered fig tree that had been alive just a few days earlier. Peter reminded them that Jesus had the power to curse it. (See Mark 11:20–21.) In response, Jesus encouraged His disciples to have faith for the impossible, saying,

> *Have faith in God. For assuredly, I say to you, whoever says to this mountain, 'Be removed and be cast into the sea,' and does not doubt in*

his heart but believes that those things he says will be done, he will have
whatever he says. Therefore I say to you, whatever things you ask when
you pray, believe that you receive them, and you will have them.

(Mark 11:22–24)

Sometimes, we look for explanations for actions that we see as unreasonable, such as cursing a fig tree. Instead, Jesus switched the focus from the cursed fig tree to the power of having faith in God. He wanted to shine the spotlight on the faith necessary to perform miracles. Something miraculous happens when we face a challenge with faith in God. We were saved by faith in Jesus, and now we can live a supernatural life of faith in Him.

He who believes in Me, the works that I do he will do also; and
greater works than these he will do, because I go to My Father. And
whatever you ask in My name, that I will do, that the Father may be
glorified in the Son. If you ask anything in My name, I will do it.

(John 14:12–14)

ACCOMPLISHING THE IMPOSSIBLE

The Bible is filled with stories of ordinary people accomplishing the impossible through faith in God. Noah was commissioned to build a ship nearly the size of a modern-day aircraft carrier by hand! The ark was an enormous boat, big enough to accommodate every kind of animal in advance of a global flood. Imagine the impossibility of even building such a boat by hand, much less gathering all the animals. Noah would never have been able to calculate those things himself, but God knew how to build the perfect boat. Noah just had to listen and obey.

Moses was eighty when he stood before a bush that blazed with God's glory. Imagine God instructing him to bring approximately two million people out of Egypt and take them to a land He had promised to Abraham more than seven hundred years earlier! Moses had many reasons to believe he was unfit for the job, including his being too old and extremely shy. Would anyone listen to him? Pharaoh would probably kill him. Even if Moses could organize the people, and even if Pharaoh allowed them to leave, how would he lead and care for two million people in a hot desert without food and water? Despite these enormous obstacles, Moses submitted to his destiny, obeyed to the best of his ability, and, with God's help, did the impossible.

Joshua and the Israelites obeyed God's directions and marched around the city of Jericho for seven days, first in silence and then, on the seventh day, offering a shout of praise to God—and the thick walls of the city came crashing down. Our God is the God of the impossible. Centuries later, Jesus explained the power of God for the miraculous to His disciples, saying, "*With men this is impossible, but with God all things are possible*" (Matthew 19:26).

Expect God to do what only He can do. We serve a supernatural God, and though we live in the natural realm, we can supersede the natural realm through faith. God's Word created the realm we call natural. Creation is solely an act of God. It is not an accident, a mistake, or the product of an inferior deity but the self-expression of God's Word. "*By faith we understand that the worlds were framed by the word of God, so that the things which are seen **were not made of things which are visible**"* (Hebrews 11:3). Creation provides evidence for the unseen, but it takes faith to believe in the unseen. It takes faith to look at the world as we know it and believe there is a Creator. With faith, you must learn to look through what is seen and perceive the unseen. And the evidence of the unseen is faith. When you trust in the Lord, He can make a way where there seems to be no way by exceeding the natural realm with one word.

The last book Oral Roberts wrote before he passed away was entitled *When You See the Invisible, You Can Do the Impossible*. Oral wrote these encouraging words for those who want to accomplish more: "God will move so mightily on you that you will not only see the invisible but also begin to do the impossible He has called you to do!"

EXPECT GOD TO DO WHAT ONLY HE CAN DO.

A MIRACLE IN PAKISTAN

When Amanda and I were in our twenties, God called us to international evangelism. He called us to go to the unreached regions of the world, the places where the lost and the hurting have never heard of the love of Jesus Christ—who didn't know that He died and rose again to give them eternal life. God showed us clearly that we were to serve Him in supernatural faith on the world's harvest fields. There were people who wholeheartedly supported us, and there were others who thought it was impossible and doubted that we could succeed. But God was faithful to His word to us.

Whether we are holding open-air crusades in a third-world country or speaking in a church in the United States, we tell the people that Jesus is not a dead God. Jesus is alive, and He wants to save them, heal them, and deliver them still today. Recently, in a crusade in Pakistan, a man named Shoquat was saved and healed of hepatitis, and his life was changed forever. I had the opportunity to talk with him after the crusade.

"I was a hepatitis patient," Shoquat began. "I suffered terribly with this illness for eight months. The doctors gave me many different tests, and I took medicine as well, but nothing helped. I was told by fellow villagers that I was under a spell.

"My sickness started as full body aches. My abdomen would get stiff, then swell and cause great pain. I suffered from severe headaches that would start without warning whether I was sitting down or up doing something else. I was a tractor driver for a man who owned his own business. But, after I got sick, I had to quit my job. I had no work, so I stayed at home all day."

At this point, Shoquat attended one of our gospel crusades in Pakistan where we were sharing the love and power of Jesus Christ to save and heal. After preaching that night, and before I prayed for the sick, I declared healing over everyone in Jesus's name. I said, "Every sickness be healed, in Jesus's name. Be healed from the top of your head to the soles of your feet. Be healed right now in the name of Jesus through the power of the Holy Spirit."

Shoquat's story continues: "As the evangelist prayed, we were told to place one hand on our head, then place our other hand on our heart. So, I did. Suddenly, my heart started beating very fast. At the same time, the hand on my head felt so heavy. Twice during the prayer, I felt like I was going to fall, but I stood my ground. And as soon as Pastor Chris said, 'Amen,' I felt like a completely new man!"

The smile that spread across Shoquat's face at that moment could have lit up a football stadium.

"I am so happy now!" he exclaimed. "I don't have the words to describe it. As soon as my previous boss heard the news, he sent someone to bring me to him. I went at six thirty this morning. When we reached his house, he asked me, 'Are you okay now?' I said, 'Yes, I am fine.' Then, my boss handed me the tractor key and said, 'Take the tractor to the tube well, then.'" "Is your boss a Muslim?" I asked him. "Yes," he replied. One more nonbeliever hearing about the love and power of Jesus Christ!

Shoquat finished his testimony with praise. "I am so grateful to Jesus Christ. I am grateful for everything. He gave me a new life. I had given up on myself. But I am very happy now." He lifted his face to the sky and his arms in praise to the living God who saw him and healed him, just as He said in His Word that He would!

In all circumstances, having faith is the key to the impossible, so have faith in God. *"But Jesus looked at them and said to them, 'With men this is impossible, but with God all things are possible'"* (Matthew 19:26).

GOD MAKES A WAY IN QATAR

In 2021, we took a ministry trip to Pakistan for a gospel crusade and faced some challenging problems with our visas. Every time we go overseas to third-world countries, there is a special procedure that is required to apply for the correct visa. We always get our visas approved, but there is never a guarantee. We went through the process as we always do. Then, on the day before leaving, we were informed that the policy had changed, and our old visa process would no longer get us into the country. We had to go through a lengthy online process to fill out all the paperwork again to apply. Thankfully, they emailed us a letter with permission to begin our travels, but it wasn't a grant for an approved visa.

The visa approval was pending, and we risked missing our window of opportunity to go. We worked into the early morning hours to get all the paperwork completed. We were told it would take up to 48 hours for a response, but we needed those visas approved in less than 24 hours! We searched for other ways to make it onto our flights that were already booked. We couldn't change flights because the next available ones would land the day after the crusade. In faith, we boarded our flight from Orlando to Qatar praying that our visas would be approved by the time we landed. But when we arrived in Qatar, the visas still had not been approved. What should we do? We had a three-hour layover before boarding our flight to Pakistan, but if we landed in Pakistan without the visas, it would be a catastrophe.

To make matters worse, we discovered that we couldn't wait for a later flight out of Qatar, after all, because our layover at the airport would last more than 24 hours. During the Covid-19 pandemic, Qatar had established a law making it *illegal* to remain in their airport for more than 24 hours. If we waited in the airport for the later flight, we would be arrested; if we went ahead and traveled without our visas, we would be denied entrance upon arrival, deported, and probably never allowed back into the country. It was an overwhelming situation, and time was of the essence. We couldn't come up with a solution on our own. Needless to say, we needed a miracle!

God had spoken to me very personally about this nation and planted within me a strong desire to bring them the gospel message. He has confirmed His word repeatedly to us in so many different crusades, so I prayed that His provision would be there for us again.

We were sitting in the airport lounge in Doha, Qatar, and they were to board the final flight to our destination country. Still, we had no visas. Then, just minutes before the plane's boarding door closed, we received an email saying our visas had been approved. I think Amanda and I both almost shouted "Hallelujah!" in that lounge.

God provided a way where there seemed to be no way. Why? Because the kingdom of hell will not prevail against the kingdom of God. God's kingdom will advance, regardless of natural circumstances. We laid hold of that promise, and we will continue laying hold of it by faith in the name of Jesus. We were committed to pushing forward in faith until God answered. By His hand, we boarded the 747 and reached our destination in time for the crusade. During the event, tens of thousands of people received Jesus Christ as their Lord and Savior. I am forever thankful for God's supernatural provision which makes the impossible possible!

TWO

FAITH BEGINS AND ENDS
WITH JESUS

"Faith is not a step into the dark, but a leap into the light."
—*Reinhard Bonnke*

"Now faith is the substance of things hoped for,
the evidence of things not seen."
—Hebrews 11:1

Faith is the key to everything in our walk with Jesus Christ—faith for our salvation, faith for our calling, and faith for activating the miraculous in our lives. Throughout the Bible, the truth of faith is like a staircase. You may intellectually know that the stairs go up to the next level, but until you climb the stairs, you won't *experience* that next level. Martin Luther King Jr. once said: "Faith is taking the first step even when you can't see the whole staircase." You can believe in the stairs and settle for knowing the stairs are there, but in order to walk in true faith, you have to climb the stairs!

The first step to having faith is understanding that faith *always begins with Jesus and always ends with Jesus.* If we don't have Jesus, we don't have a firm foundation. With Jesus, you can do anything. With Jesus, you can overcome any obstacle in life! He is the Author and the Finisher of our faith. (See Hebrews 12:2.) All of our faith is found in Him.

"Now faith is the substance of things hoped for, the evidence [elegchos] of things not seen" (Hebrews 11:1). The Greek Word *elegchos* means proof, conviction, evidence, a thing proved or tested.[3] *"Now faith is"*—the author is emphasizing the reality of faith, a living, continuing, daily reality, where we can take God at His word. Faith is the structural foundation and convicting evidence, making God's promises a reality in our lives each day. Faith is what God provides to add substance—something concrete—to what we believe and yet do not see. And true faith has its beginning in Jesus.

> THE FIRST STEP TO HAVING FAITH IS UNDERSTANDING THAT FAITH ALWAYS BEGINS WITH JESUS AND ALWAYS ENDS WITH JESUS.

IN THE BEGINNING WAS THE WORD

"In the beginning was the Word [logos], and the Word was with God, and the Word was God" (John 1:1). If you didn't know, you might question, "Who is the Word?" John answers that question by declaring that the

3. Blue Letter Bible online, *elegchos*, https://www.blueletterbible.org/lexicon/g1650/kjv/tr/0-1/.

Word (*logos*) is Jesus. "*And the Word* [*logos*] *became flesh and dwelt among us, and we beheld His glory, the glory as of the only begotten from the Father, full of grace and truth*" (John 1:14). The Greek word *logos* in this passage is commonly translated as *word*. But to the Jewish and Gentile readers, who were familiar with *logos*, it also referred to the entire communication process of God, and the written word of God (the Scriptures).[4] By divine revelation, John writes that *logos* is the word that fully reveals Jesus Christ—*the eternal Word of God*. When John introduces Jesus with the term *logos*, his readers realize that he is describing Jesus as being present "*in the beginning*" before creation, before time began.

Jesus was not only present at creation, but He was also responsible for the creation, along with the Father and the Holy Spirit. We see this in the opening verses of Genesis 1:1–3: "*In the beginning God created the heavens and the earth. Now the earth was formless and empty, darkness was over the surface of the deep, and the Spirit of God was hovering over the waters. And God said, 'Let there be light,' and there was light*" (NIV). When we compare these verses from the first chapters of Genesis and John, we can clearly see who was present at creation: the Father, the Word, and the Spirit—the Trinity.

For his Jewish readers, by introducing Jesus as the *Word*, John points them back to the Old Testament, where the Hebrew word *babar* is translated as *Word* and is associated with the personification of God's revelation and an instrument for the execution of God's will.[5] The Old Testament says, "*By the word* [*babar*] *of the* LORD *the heavens were made, and all the host of them by the breath of His mouth*" (Psalm 33:6). "*He sent His word and healed them, and delivered them from their destructions*" (Psalm 107:20). "*Forever, O* LORD, *Your word is settled in heaven*" (Psalm 119:89). "*He sends out His word, and melts them; He causes His wind to blow, and the waters flow*" (Psalm 147:18).

---

4. BibleHub.com, c.f. *Logos*, Topical Bible: Logos (biblehub.com).
5. Jeff A. Benner, "Word," Ancient Hebrew Research Center, Hebrew Word Definition: Word | AHRC (ancient-hebrew.org).

The Bible does not say that God created the Word; it says, "Jesus *is* the Word." Why? Because Jesus is the uncreated Son of God. And because Jesus has created all things, He is the one who created faith in the first place! You can put your faith in Jesus because He alone is the reason we can have supernatural faith. As you meditate on the life of Jesus and the influence His words had on the people He encountered, you will be motivated to walk by faith in the power of those words, realizing every promise in the Bible was spoken by Jesus. When Jesus took on human flesh, the Father and the Holy Spirit watched over Him and raised an army of disciples empowered by faith to change the world in Jesus's name. If you have God's faith, you can overcome any situation, any storm you're going through, and any obstacle in life. Jesus is the beginning of faith!

THE FAITH OF GOD WITHIN US

"Without faith it is impossible to please God, because anyone who comes to God must believe that he exists and that he rewards those who earnestly seek him" (Hebrews 11:6 NIV). Our relationship with God depends on faith. Faith brings the things God has provided for us from the spiritual realm into the physical realm. (See Hebrews 11:1.) Our faith is the victory that enables us to overcome the world. *"For whatever is born of God overcomes the world. And this is the victory that has overcome the world— our faith"* (1 John 5:4). Everything God does for us is accessed through faith. But it is not *our* faith. It is the faith of God within us.

In Ephesians 2:8, Paul writes, *"For by grace you have been **saved through faith**, and that not of yourselves; **it is the gift of God**."* We must put faith in God's grace, but the faith that we use isn't our own human faith. This verse says that our faith is *"the gift of God."* We are each given a certain amount of faith. As the apostle Paul explains it, *"God hath dealt to every man **the measure of faith**"* (Romans 12:3 KJV). God didn't give us different measures of faith; we all received *"the"* measure of faith, which is the *faith of God*. *"And Jesus answering, saith to them: Have* [the] *faith of God"* (Mark 11:22 YLT).

OUR RELATIONSHIP WITH GOD DEPENDS ON FAITH. FAITH BRINGS THE THINGS GOD HAS PROVIDED
FOR US FROM THE SPIRITUAL REALM INTO THE PHYSICAL REALM.

Many times, when we think of faith, we think we need more faith as if we don't have enough to begin with. The truth is that you already have enough faith if you have the faith of God. The Bible tells us that even if you have the smallest measure of faith, you can move mountains and that nothing will be impossible for you. Jesus said, *"For assuredly, I say to you, if you have faith as a mustard seed, you will say to this mountain, 'Move from here to there,' and it will move; and nothing will be impossible for you"* (Matthew 17:20). Jesus is clearly telling us that it's not a matter of the size of your faith, stating that even if you have a very small amount of faith—faith the size of a tiny mustard seed—you have enough faith to do anything impossible. Praise God!

My friend, it's not a matter of needing more faith. You already have the supernatural faith of Jesus. Now you just need to learn how to activate it, and that's exactly what you're going to learn in this book. God wants to use you in the miraculous, and you will fulfill your call by faith in Jesus's name.

There are Christians who think they are living "by faith" based on what they see, but that is not faith at all. The Bible tells us that supernatural faith is based on what we do not see. Romans 4:17 says, *"God…calls those things which do not exist as though they did."* God's faith goes beyond sight. God's faith operates supernaturally, beyond the limitations of our natural faith.

Andrew Wommack, evangelist and Bible teacher, writes, "There is much confusion about faith today just as there has always been. It's like having a computer and knowing its potential but not having a clue how to use it. Many of us have experienced this, and we know how frustrating it can be! The Bible is our manual with detailed instructions, but just like we ignore other manuals in the natural, few people take the time to study God's Word. They are impatient and want to do it on their own. They may reach some level of Christian success, but to be proficient, they must read the Book."[6] Womack continues by saying that one area of faith that gives people the most trouble is the misconception that we must acquire *more faith* and that some people have much faith while others have virtually none. We spend a lot of effort, "like a dog chasing its tail," trying to get something we already have. Every born-again Christian already has the same quality and quantity of faith that Jesus has given us.

FAITH TO REDEEM US

I am so thankful for the faith that God gives us. That faith transformed my life forever!

I grew up in a great home on a dairy farm in central Minnesota. My parents, Gerald and Virginia Mikkelson, have run that farm for over fifty years, and still have it today. I am the youngest child of three, and my parents took me to church every Sunday until I was eighteen. I knew all about God growing up, going to Sunday school and Bible studies, and even leading the occasional Bible study. But in

---

6. Andrew Wommack Ministries, "Faith of God," https://www.awmi.net/reading/teaching-articles/faith_god/.

my heart, my faith was weak, and I had hidden sin in my life. Slowly my desire for the world grew stronger and my relationship with the Lord grew weaker to the point of nonexistence. By the time I was a freshman in college, I was getting drunk regularly and experimenting with drugs.

After two years of college, I dropped out—but I was still the life of the party! I could no longer afford the drugs I was using, so I thought, "Why not sell them and use the money to buy what I want?" My life was spiraling out of control, but I kept pushing forward without Jesus. I moved to Minneapolis for a new job and took my sin right along with me. I owned a racing motorcycle, and I soon found a group of men and women who shared my passion for riding this type of bike. They quickly became like family to me. Our goal in life was to have as much fun as possible; we raced our bikes on the highways near Minneapolis, sometimes flying down the road at 160 miles per hour or doing wheelies at 100 mph! (I'm so thankful for God's protection during those wild days!) My life was a mess, and I was in major bondage to sin. I was running from God and running toward my sinful, fleshly desires. This lifestyle led me down a dark path that seemed like fun on the surface but left me empty inside.

My biker buddies and I—sometimes thirty-five of us at a time—would meet at a coffee shop every day after work. Then I would gas up my bike at the service station right next to the coffee shop. Every time I went into the service station, I saw the pretty blonde girl who worked there. Her name was Amanda—yes, you guessed it, she's now my beautiful wife. In the beginning, Amanda and I partied together all the time and lived a sinful, worldly life. But inside there was still a haunting feeling that something was very wrong. I was in my mid-twenties, and my life was going nowhere.

I AM SO THANKFUL FOR THE FAITH THAT GOD GIVES US. THAT FAITH TRANSFORMED MY LIFE FOREVER!

FAITH IN JESUS CHANGED EVERYTHING

One day, Amanda startled me by asking if I would go to church with her. She hadn't grown up in in a Christian family, but her sister had been radically saved and had invited her to church. (Amanda's entire family has since been saved.) Amanda expected me to say, "No way!" But I was actually intrigued and responded, "Sure, I'll go." She was shocked! She knew nothing about my past and thought that church was the furthest thing from my mind.

That Sunday morning, we heard a great message. At the end of the service, the pastor invited the congregation to a special service on Wednesday night for the parents of children who were caught up in drugs and alcohol. Funny thing Amanda and I only heard the words "Come to the special Wednesday night service." The Holy Spirit must have blocked out the part about parents of children doing drugs! -

When we walked into church that Wednesday night, we realized to our horror that it was a meeting just for parents of teens who were living our kind of lifestyle. We didn't want to be rude and walk out, so we just sat in the back to stay out of the way. While the pastor was ministering to the parents, the Holy Spirit was ministering to us in the back of the church. The pastor started talking about the desperate life of drugs and alcohol, and the Holy Spirit began convicting me so strongly. Amanda had never been in a church where you could feel the presence of God, and she sat beside me with tears streaming down her face. When we got in the car after the service, she turned to me and said, "Chris, I want to serve God. If you don't want to be with me, I don't care. I want to serve God." I looked at her and said, "Amanda, I want to serve God, too." And that night we made the most important decision of our lives. We decided to start following Jesus.

When we walked into the apartment after the service, we saw that our partying friends had trashed the place, and I recognized the ugliness of sin. I was living halfway for God for about two months, until the moment came that I realized it was not enough, and I spoke these words out loud: "God, I'm done. I'm all in. I don't care if people don't like me. I don't care if my friends laugh at me. All I want is to live my life 100 percent for You." Praise God, we met Jesus, and He transformed our lives forever. Not long after, Amanda and I were married; our faith in Jesus changed *everything*! That was the first step on our journey of faith where Jesus set our hearts free and eventually set us on fire for evangelizing the nations. When you put your faith in Jesus Christ, He makes your way straight.

CALLED FOR LIFE

Several years later, God called me to be an international evangelist, to go to the unreached and outermost parts of the world, especially to countries where the people have never heard the gospel—the account of Jesus Christ's life, death, and resurrection to give them eternal life. Amanda and I were still in our twenties when God showed us that we were to serve Him together on the world's harvest fields. Amanda is the "Swiss army knife" in our ministry, traveling world-wide, serving as administrator, and supporting our call in every way possible. Our obedience to God's call has enabled us to experience countless miracles.

Early in our ministry in Pakistan, Amanda and I walked onto the platform one day and saw a sea of people who had been eagerly waiting for us to arrive and preach the gospel. What thrilled us the most was that we knew most of the people in attendance were not

Christians. In fact, when I made the altar call for salvation after my message, I was careful to tell those who were already Christians that they didn't need to stand to receive salvation again. Since everyone was sitting, I asked that only those who had never received Jesus before to stand. What we saw next was unbelievable! Thousands of people stood to their feet. From the stage, it looked like between 70 and 80 percent of those gathered had just received Jesus Christ as their Lord and Savior for the very first time. Hallelujah! Since that time, this has become a common occurrence in Pakistan. We often see upwards of three-fourths of the crowd coming to Jesus in a dark and difficult land. Praise God! And wherever we minister the gospel, there are local pastors who follow up with the new believers and help them to plug into a local church for discipleship.

It thrills my soul to see so many people come to Jesus. I have never lose my sense of awe at what Jesus is doing. This is what it's all about. I love to preach in churches and minister to Christians, and I love to see people be healed and delivered. However, what I really long for is being on dusty fields in foreign lands, preaching the cross and seeing thousands of people come to faith in Jesus Christ.

That night, after leading the people in a prayer for salvation, I briefly taught on the baptism of the Holy Spirit and gave everyone an opportunity to be filled with the power of the Holy Spirit. It was a glorious sight—thousands of people all over the field were noticeably being touched and filled. Then, I prayed for the sick, and Jesus did mighty miracles. Bones, backs, and legs were healed in Jesus's name. One man wore homemade casts of white cotton wrapped around wooden rulers on both his wrists. I asked him why the doctors hadn't put proper casts on his broken wrists, and he told me that he couldn't afford to pay for them. But that night, the goodness of God was on full display. The Lord Jesus touched his wrists and healed both of them. Praise God!

I HAVE NEVER LOSE MY SENSE OF AWE AT WHAT JESUS IS DOING. THIS IS WHAT IT'S ALL ABOUT.

FAITH FOR HEALING

During a crusade a couple of years later, we met a Muslim woman who had traveled over eight hours to come to our gospel campaign. She had severe medical problems that caused constant, excruciating pain all over her body. The woman had seen many doctors who tried many different methods and medicines to heal her. But they couldn't figure out what was wrong with her, and she continued getting worse. Because she was in constant pain, her Muslim friends encouraged her to see a witch doctor. Thankfully, before she followed their advice, she saw an advertisement on Pakistani television for one of our gospel campaigns and heard that Jesus Christ heals people in our meetings.

She decided to travel by bus to join our open-air meeting in hopes of receiving a healing that night. After she heard the good news about Jesus, she received Him as her Lord and Savior. As soon as I prayed for the sick, God touched her, and she felt all the pain leave her body. What the doctors hadn't been able to fix in countless appointments over many years, Jesus fixed in just a moment. God is the Great Physician who touched her body that night and completely healed her. She stood on the stage and testified that from that night forward, she would follow Jesus Christ as her Lord and Savior.

There are so many other testimonies I could share, but I am rejoicing over the greatest testimony of all—the testimony of thousands who have now gone from darkness to light, from bondage to freedom, from sin to salvation, and from death to light, in Jesus's name.

FAITH IS THE KEY

Nothing works without faith, for faith is the key. This entire book is about having faith in God. That's why I love Hebrews, chapter 11, and I especially love reading about the men in the Bible, real human beings who had great faith in God, such as Noah, Abraham, and Moses.

By faith Noah, being divinely warned of things not yet seen, moved with godly fear, prepared an ark for the saving of his household, by which he condemned the world and became heir of the righteousness which is according to faith.   (Hebrews 11:7)

By faith Abraham obeyed when he was called to go out to the place which he would receive as an inheritance. And he went out, not knowing where he was going. By faith, he dwelt in the land of promise as in a foreign country, dwelling in tents with Isaac and Jacob, the heirs with him of the same promise; for he waited for the city which has foundations, whose builder and maker is God.
                          (Hebrews 11:8–10)

By faith Moses, when he was born, was hidden three months by his parents, because they saw he was a beautiful child; and they were not afraid of the king's command. By faith Moses, when he became of age, refused to be called the son of Pharaoh's daughter, choosing rather to suffer affliction with the people of God than enjoy the passing pleasures of sin, esteeming the reproach of Christ greater riches than the treasures in Egypt; for he looked to the reward. By faith he forsook Egypt, not fearing the wrath of the king; for he endured as seeing Him who is invisible. By faith he kept the Passover and the sprinkling of blood, lest he who destroyed the firstborn should touch them. By faith they passed through the Red Sea as by dry

land, whereas the Egyptians, attempting to do so, were drowned.
(Hebrews 11:23–29)

Our faith is established by confessing that Jesus is the Christ, the Son of God. *"For whatever is born of God overcomes the world. And this is the victory that has overcome the world, our faith"* (1 John 5:4). Those born of God overcome the world, rising above their storms like an eagle. When all other birds flee from the storm and hide from its fierceness, eagles fly into it and will use the wind and pressure of the storm to glide higher without having to use their energy; they fly above the storm. The Holy Spirit is the wind that lifts us above our storms, and the pressure is the faith that engages the power of God to overcome. By faith you can climb higher than any storm, you can move any mountain, you can overcome any obstacle—not because of your intellect, talent, strength, or charisma, but because of faith in Jesus Christ. When you have faith in Jesus, anything is possible. All things are possible to them that believe in Jesus. Then you can say, with the apostle Paul, *"I can do all things through Christ who strengthens me"* (Philippians 4:13).

PUT YOUR FAITH IN JESUS

When you put your faith in Jesus, He will start blessing you in ways you never would have imagined. True faith must begin and end with Jesus Christ. It's all about Jesus. You might be in the middle of a storm in your life. Maybe there are circumstances around you that are shaking your world right now. I want to tell you that you can trust Jesus. You can trust Him! He's there with you amid the storms of life! Today, right now, you can call out to Jesus, and He will answer! Faith begins with Jesus, and it ends with Jesus! You can trust that He is a firm foundation.

If you don't yet know Jesus, there's no better time to get to know Him. He's waiting for you right now. Jesus says in Revelation 3:20, *"Behold, I stand at the door and knock. If anyone hears My voice and opens the door, I will come in to him and dine with him, and he with Me."* Jesus is waiting at the door of your heart, and He's knocking even now. But Jesus will never break down the door to get in. He waits like a gentleman for you to open that door. You might say, "Chris, my life is a mess. I don't think God loves me or that He can save me. I've made too many mistakes." If God can save a sinner like me, I promise that He is more than able to save you. He loves you. You're the reason Jesus came to earth. Even if you were the only person alive, He would have come and died just for you.

*IF YOU DON'T YET KNOW JESUS,
THERE'S NO BETTER TIME TO GET TO KNOW HIM.*

Open the door to Jesus now. Repent of your sin. Turn away from your old life and turn to Jesus. Ask Jesus to save you, and He will save you even now. Romans 10:9–10 assures us,

If you confess with your mouth the Lord Jesus and believe in your heart that God has raised Him from the dead, you will be saved. For with the heart one believes unto righteousness, and with the mouth confession is made unto salvation.

If you know your heart isn't right with God, and you recognize your need for His forgiveness and salvation, the Bible says God's promise is for you to be saved. All you need to do is believe in Jesus. Believe that He died and rose from the dead for you, and confess this with your mouth.

Pray this prayer out loud right now: "Heavenly Father, I come to You in the mighty name of Jesus, and I confess that I'm a sinner. I repent of all my sins. I want to follow You. I want to know You and Your saving power. I believe that Jesus Christ is the Son of God, that He died for my sins, and that He rose from the dead. Please forgive me now. Fill me with Your Holy Spirit and make me brand new. From this day forward, I will follow You for the rest of my life. In Jesus's name, I pray. Amen!"

Praise God! My friend, if you prayed that prayer with me, I want to be the first person to congratulate you and welcome you into the family of God. God loves you so much and has an amazing plan for your life. According to the Bible, your sins are washed away as far as the east is from the west. (See Psalm 103:12.) You are now a new person in Christ. The old person is gone, and Jesus has made you brand new. *"Therefore, if anyone is in Christ, he is a new creation; old things have passed away; behold, all things have become new"* (2 Corinthians 5:17). Just as He changed my life, He will change yours for your good and His glory.

Jesus is the starting gate for all things in faith. Jesus is the beginning of faith, and Jesus is the end of faith. Your faith in Him is the beginning of a life of supernatural living. He will do things in and through you that you could only dream about. Keep your eyes on Jesus and watch what He will do through you!

THREE

FAITH IN THE WORD, NOT CIRCUMSTANCES

"Faith has nothing to do with feelings or with impressions, with improbabilities or with outward experiences. If we desire to couple such things with faith, then we are no longer resting on the Word of God, because faith needs nothing of the kind. Faith rests on the naked Word of God. When we take Him at His Word, the heart is at peace."[7]
—*George Mueller*

"For we walk by faith, not by sight."
—2 Corinthians 5:7

Faith rests on the naked Word of God." George Mueller was a man of great faith, and he knew what he was talking about. Great faith is not

---

7. Bible Portal, "Inspirational Quotes by George Mueller," bibleportal.com/bible-quotes/author/George-Mueller.

based on feelings or past experiences. Faith is based solely on the Word of God.

There is a captivating account of the disciples on a boat in the middle of a choppy sea that contains the greatest act of faith by one of Jesus's disciples. While they're in the middle of the sea, suddenly, a terrible storm comes up. Fear grips their hearts as they battle the wind, waves, and heavy rain around them. Unexpectedly, they see what looks like a ghost walking on the water toward them. Let's read the account in Matthew 14 of Peter walking on the water.

> *Now in the fourth watch of the night Jesus went to them, walking on the sea. And when the disciples saw Him walking on the sea, they were troubled, saying, "It is a ghost!" And they cried out for fear. But immediately Jesus spoke to them, saying, "Be of good cheer! It is I; do not be afraid." And Peter answered Him and said, "Lord, if it is You, command me to come to You on the water." So He said, "Come." And when Peter had come down out of the boat, he walked on the water to go to Jesus.* (Matthew 14:25–29)

When I think about great faith, I always think of this story of Peter walking on the water. What kind of faith would it take a person to step out of a perfectly good boat in the middle of a stormy sea—especially someone like Peter, who had been a fisherman by trade for most of his life? According to the disciples' reactions, this was a violent storm, and these fishermen were caught in a harrowing situation. Usually, the focus of this Bible account is that Peter started to sink when he took his eyes off of Jesus. (We'll look at that detail a little later.) But right now, I want to focus on the faith that Peter had to stand on Jesus's word and *step out of that boat and start walking on the surface of the water.*

I can imagine the scene that windy night on the Sea of Galilee. Peter standing on the side of the wooden boat with the storm raging and seeing Jesus out on the water. The boat was tossing back and forth by the waves, but when Peter stepped out of the boat, something super-natural happened: a miracle was activated. Peter walked on water. He began doing the impossible as the water held his weight, all because of one word from Jesus: *"Come."*

When I was in Bible school many years ago, God revealed something powerful to me about this account of Peter walking on water. The Lord showed me that, yes, Peter was miraculously walking on water, but he wasn't just walking on water; he was *standing on the Word of God.* Jesus said one word to Peter—*"Come"*—and with that one word, Peter stepped out of the boat and walked toward Jesus. Every step Peter took, he heard the word *"Come," "Come," Come,"* because he was standing on the Word of God. Jesus spoke only *one word,* but that one word changed Peter's life forever. His faith wasn't in the water but *in Jesus's Word.*

Remember, Jesus Christ is the Son of God, but He is also the Word (*logos*) of God, who became flesh and dwelt among us! Jesus Christ is God, and His words are eternal. He is the Ancient of Days, the Word of God who lived among us and died for us! His words are eternal, and His words are life. Again, Jesus is the same Word who spoke in Genesis 1:3, *"Let there be light."* He is the same Word who spoke, *"Let Us make man in Our image, according to Our likeness"* (Genesis 1:26). That same Jesus *spoke,* and His Word stirred Peter to step out of the boat in faith and begin walking.

When Jesus speaks, you can stand on His Word! Jesus says, *"Most assuredly, I say to you, he who **hears My word** and believes in Him who sent Me has everlasting life, and shall not come into judgment, but has passed from death into life"* (John 5:24). Peter stepped out in supernatural faith and began walking on water. If you want great faith, make sure your faith is standing on the Word of God.

JESUS SPOKE ONLY ONE WORD, BUT THAT ONE WORD CHANGED PETER'S LIFE FOREVER.

FAITH FOR MIRACLES

That night on the sea, Peter stepped into the realm of the miraculous. It was miraculous because he believed in the Word and then had the faith to step out in it. Hebrews 11:1 confirms that faith is not based on circumstances or feelings: *"Now faith is the substance of things hoped for, the evidence [elegchos] of things not seen."* Remember, the Greek word *elegchos* means conviction. Therefore, faith is a convicting force that propels you to believe in God and His Word even though you haven't seen God with your own eyes. In the same way, a judge and jury will convict a criminal based on evidence for something that they didn't witness but are convinced took place. We can have conviction in God and His Word that causes us to act and move by faith, even though we don't see God in the natural.

With Jesus's command to come, Peter displayed an immovable faith that was a rock-solid conviction in his spirit. It was *Jesus* walking on water, not a ghost. In Peter's spirit, he knew that it was Jesus, and he was confident that he could do whatever Jesus wanted him to do. The power of conviction causes us to be willing to step into the spiritual realm and do the impossible. Peter had his eyes on Jesus because all faith must start with Him. Again, it needs to be emblazoned in our soul: Faith starts with Jesus, and it ends with Jesus.

Jesus was the chosen One sent with power and authority from the Father. Every experience the disciples encountered with Jesus revealed Him as God and built their faith in preparation for the moment when Jesus would no longer be with them in person. Having been with Jesus and seeing His power, Peter knew that Jesus could do the impossible—the supernatural! Jesus demonstrated that He was in command of the natural elements as only God can be. Revealing this truth to the disciples was a witness to His divinity; they responded with a confession of faith in Jesus as God by worshiping Him. *"Then those who were in the boat came and worshiped Him, saying, 'Truly You are the Son of God'"* (Matthew 14:33).

I don't care what storm may be happening around me. There could be waves tossing on one side of the boat, while it appears to be capsizing on the other side. I don't care what situation I find myself in. All I care about is Jesus. And when you're going through a storm, all you should look to is Jesus. Those looking to Jesus will have great faith that stands on the Word of God. Maybe you're in a storm right now, a physical storm of sickness. Maybe there's a miracle you're waiting for because of illness and pain. Maybe it's a financial crisis, a marital issue, or a relationship breakdown in your family. Whatever it is, when you are in a storm, don't look to other people for the answer. Look only to Jesus. Release every burden to Him and *"run with endurance…, looking unto Jesus, the author and finisher of our faith…"* (Hebrews 12:1–2).

Those who look only to Jesus will have great faith that stands on the Word of God. Peter was in the middle of a storm walking on water *because* he was looking at Jesus, responding to that one word, *"Come."* Again, Peter's faith came from the Word of God. Romans 10:17 says, *"So then faith comes by hearing, and hearing by the word of God."* Peter knew that if Jesus called to him to come, he could come and stand on the water. Amid a terrible storm, Peter chose to stand on Jesus's Word and not on the circumstances surrounding him. We each need to stand on the Word if Jesus says to us, *"Come."*

*FAITH IS A CONVICTING FORCE THAT PROPELS
YOU TO BELIEVE IN GOD AND HIS WORD
EVEN THOUGH YOU HAVEN'T SEEN GOD
WITH YOUR OWN EYES.*

RESPOND IN FAITH TO THE WORD

We have all been guilty of putting our faith in our circumstances and situations. Perhaps, in times of illness, you have assumed that God doesn't want to heal you, even though there are hundreds of verses in His Word on healing. Too many people put their faith in circumstances and what is going wrong around them rather than trusting and acting on the Word of God. Peter realized something powerful that became a part of his walk with Jesus. Peter's life and ministry were just beginning to be built on the Word of God. God's Word will never fail. God's Word is always true. His Word is a firm foundation. That is how Peter, by standing on the Word, activated a miracle and began walking in the supernatural.

In a way, Abraham had an experience similar to Peter's in learning to trust in God's Word. In Genesis, we read that Abraham walked by faith according to the word God spoke to him. The Lord said to Abraham, back when he was still called Abram, *"Get out of your country, from your family and from your father's house, to a land that I will show you. I will make you a great nation; I will bless you and make your name great"* (Genesis 12:1–2). Abraham did not act according to his circumstances; instead, trusting in God's Word, he agreed to go to a place he did not know. It's interesting that Peter's word from Jesus was essentially to *come* while Abraham's word from God was to *go*. Whatever the circumstances, we must respond in faith to the Word of God.

Years later, Abraham responded once again by faith in God's Word. Genesis 15:4 reads, *"Behold, the Word of the LORD came to him, saying, 'This one shall not be your heir, but one who will come from your own body shall be your heir.'"* Though Abraham was one hundred years old, he believed that the Word of the Lord was true. The Bible confirms that God's Word was greater than Abraham's circumstances: *"And not being weak in faith, he did not consider his own body, already dead (since he was about a hundred years old), and the deadness of Sarah's womb. He did not waver at the promise of God through unbelief, but was strengthened in faith, giving glory to God"* (Romans 4:19–20).

FAITH COMES BY HEARING

The Bible is clear on how we receive faith. *"So then faith [peitho] comes by hearing [akoé], and hearing by the word [rhema] of God"* (Romans 10:17). Let's unlock the meaning of these three words in the original Greek: *faith, hearing,* and the *Word.*

The Greek word *peitho,* and its derived noun *pistis,* are possibly the signature words of the Greek New Testament. The verb *peitho* means *to persuade* or *to be persuaded,* and the noun *pistis* means *faith, trust,* or *certainty.* From the noun comes the equally important verb *pisteou,* which means *to have faith* and behave as someone who has been *convinced into certainty.*[8] Faith means trusting in God and His Word with conviction and certainty.

The next Greek word, *akoé,* means *hearing sound* or our ability *to hear.* However, being able to hear alone doesn't produce faith. God speaks the truth, and you must listen attentively with your heart to believe God's Word and then choose to have faith in Him. *Akoé* can also be defined as "an inner spiritual hearing."[9]

---

8. Abarim Publications, Faith, Persuasion and Belief ;https://www.abarim-publications.com/DictionaryG/p/p-e-i-th-om.html
9. Ibid

The final Greek definition is of the *Word*, referring to the Word of God. There are two Greek words used in the Bible to refer to the word of God. The first is *logos*, which, as we already understand, refers to the written Word of God in the Scriptures and also refers to Jesus Himself. The other Greek word is *rhema*, the spoken Word of God. In Romans 10:17, Paul uses the word *rhema*, the spoken Word: "*...and hearing by the word [rhema] of God.*" We know that God will not speak a word that contradicts His written Word, the Scriptures, so there is a built-in safeguard to prevent misinterpretation. In John 8:47, Jesus says, "*Whoever belongs to God hears [akoé] what God says [rhema]. The reason you do not hear [akoé] is that you do not belong to God*" (NIV).

FAITH TO SPEAK OUT

Sadly, an erroneous idea permeates Christian thought—that our deeds will speak what we don't preach, making us believe we don't always need to use words to preach the gospel. But that is not true. Paul was clear when he wrote,

> How then shall they call on Him in whom they have not believed? And how shall they believe in Him of whom **they have not heard?** And how shall they hear without a preacher? And how shall they preach unless they are sent? (Romans 10:14–15)

Just a few verses later, Paul reminds us that faith comes by hearing and *only* by hearing God's Word. (See Romans 10:17.)

A perfect example is on the day of Pentecost when Peter spoke powerfully, applying history and biblical truth, quoting Joel and David, and testifying about what he had seen and heard from Jesus Christ. The large Jerusalem crowd he addressed heard the gospel truth by Peter's preaching, and "*about three thousand souls*" (Acts 2:41) were saved that day! You need to speak the Word so that others will hear the Word and acquire faith in God.

NO MATTER WHAT YOU'RE GOING THROUGH,
YOU CAN STAND ON GOD'S WORD AND
WALK ON HIS WORD.

When you read the Scriptures, you can trust God's Word and stand on it by faith. No matter what you're going through, you can stand on God's Word and walk on His Word. God's Word is your firm foundation. In Matthew 24:35, Jesus promises, *"Heaven and earth will pass away, but My words will by no means pass away."* In the Sermon on the Mount, Jesus closes His message with the story of a man who built his house on the sand and another man who built his house on the rock. Jesus explains that the man who hears His words and doesn't do them is like a man who built his house on the sand, not having a firm foundation. Jesus continues by saying that when the storm came, the house fell, and *"great was its fall"* (Matthew 7:27). But the man who hears the Word of God and acts on it is like the man who built his house on the rock: *"and the rain descended, the floods came, and the winds blew and beat on that house; and it did not fall, for it was founded on the rock"* (verse 25).

When the storms of life come, know that you can stand on the Word of God. Put your faith in His Word, not in the circumstances around you. Put your faith in His Word, not in your past experiences. When you hear the Word and obey, you are building on a firm foundation.

SMITH WIGGLESWORTH'S LIFE OF FAITH

Smith Wigglesworth, a British evangelist in the early 1900s, was known as the "apostle of faith," whose powerful ministry led to the foundation of the modern Pentecostal movement. His anointed messages were followed by supernatural signs and wonders, including fourteen confirmed accounts of people being raised from the dead.

"In one case, Wigglesworth went to the home of a family mourning the death of their little boy, just five years old. Tears ran down Wigglesworth's face as he looked at the boy lying in the coffin. He asked the family to leave the room, then lifted the boy's body and propped it up in a corner of the room. Rebuking death in the name of Jesus Christ, he commanded death to surrender its victim. As he prayed and stood on God's Word, the boy returned to life again!"[10] Hallelujah! Supernatural signs such as this followed Wigglesworth's ministry everywhere he went.

Wigglesworth was a man of incredible faith and power. Thousands testified to being healed as a result of his prayers of faith. Broken bodies were mended, the paralyzed walked again, cancerous tumors disappeared, in the name of Jesus. His life exuded the power of God manifested in ways few have ever seen. He once declared, "I am not moved by what I see. I am moved only by what I believe. I know this— no man looks at appearances if he believes. No man considers how he feels if he believes. The man who believes God has it."[11]

While waiting at a train station to leave for Scotland, Wigglesworth received word that his beloved wife, Polly, had collapsed at the Bowland Street Mission from a heart attack. He rushed to her bedside only to discover that her spirit had already departed. Heartbroken, he rebuked death, and she came back. Wigglesworth had just a short time to visit with his wife before the Holy Spirit impressed upon him that it was time for her to go home to be with her Lord and Savior, so he released her again. Polly passed away on January 1, 1913. From that day

10. Cheryl Elton, "Living in the Miraculous: Smith Wigglesworth—Part 1," January 7, 2018, Cheryl Elton: Living in His Presence, https://www.cherylelton.com/living-in-the-miraculous-smith-wigglesworth-part-1/.
11. GoodReads.com, "Smith Wigglesworth Quotes," https://www.goodreads.com/author/quotes/191049.Smith_Wigglesworth.

forward, it was as if her life and dedication to the Lord propelled Smith Wigglesworth to accomplish great things for Jesus.

We can't be moved by what we see, by our emotions, or by the circumstances surrounding us. You might have been praying for sickness to go away for years, asking, "What's happening? Why haven't I received my healing yet?" Don't put your faith in what you see or don't see, and don't put your faith in your experience. Put your faith in the Word of God because it is a firm foundation. Since the Bible says, *"By His stripes we are healed"* (Isaiah 53:5), you can stand on those words! First Peter 2:24 says that "[Jesus] *Himself bore our sins in His own body on the tree, that we, having died to sins, might live for righteousness—by whose stripes you were healed."* If the Bible says, *"I can do all things through Christ who strengthens me"* (Philippians 4:13), then stand on that Word and don't allow anything else in life to persuade you differently.

WE CAN'T BE MOVED BY WHAT WE SEE, BY OUR EMOTIONS, OR BY THE CIRCUMSTANCES SURROUNDING US.

STANDING ON THE WORD IN PAKISTAN

I will never forget our first trip to Pakistan more than a decade ago. Pakistan is not a place most people want to travel to because of how dangerous it is for Christians. I personally love the country and the people there. However, Pakistan is a very hostile and dangerous country to visit. Remember that U.S. Navy SEALs went to Pakistan to kill

Osama Bin Laden years after 9/11 because he was living there, hiding in a compound near Islamabad, Pakistan's capital city. Danger from extremists was the situation in Pakistan then and still today.

On that first ministry trip, I was a guest at another evangelist's crusade and went there on a scouting trip for our future ministry. While there, I preached in several churches and at several pastors' conferences. I clearly remember the first night of the gospel festival. Thousands of people were gathered on a small field to hear the message, but we couldn't drive our vehicle to the back of the stage. Normally, because of anti-Christian sentiment, the visiting evangelist will have a getaway car by the stage in case of an emergency. But given the way the field was laid out, there was no way for us to get there. So, the driver dropped us off at the back of the crowd to walk down the center aisle through the throng of people to get to the stage.

There I was, fresh from the U.S., standing behind this teeming crowd with the stage on the far side of the field. While walking to the front, I noticed that behind the stage was a tall brick building with a guy walking along the edge of the roof carrying a large gun. The crusade organizer had hired a local security company for this event, which is very common in Pakistan. Even today, we hire over sixty security guards armed with machine guns surrounding the entire perimeter to ensure everyone's safety. All the people who come must enter through one main entrance and pass through metal detectors to guarantee no one is carrying bombs or guns into the open-air event.

That first night, the more I focused on that armed guard, the more nervous I became about the security company hired for the evening. At that time in Pakistan, they didn't have Christian security companies as they do today. Therefore, the security team hired to protect us were likely not believers, since less than 2 percent of the population in Pakistan are Christians. The crusade team didn't have enough money to hire properly dressed security guards, so the security team members were dressed in normal Pakistani attire, including turbans on their heads. There was nothing to identify them as guards other than those large guns.

I realized I had no way of knowing whether these guys were members of our security team or just some random men with weapons. Since the security guards were not Christians, how was I supposed to know if they would approve of the message we preached at the crusade? How could I trust that radical terrorists had not paid them off to take us out? I was scheduled to give the short opening message that night, and I couldn't help thinking that I might not be alive to hear the end of my message!

As we walked down the aisle, the people were singing, clapping, and dancing. But my eyes remained fixed on the building behind the stage. The turbaned man on the roof was holding his gun up in the air and whirling around—he was dancing! I thought, "Oh, Lord, I pray that he's one of our security officers and that he's on our side." At that moment, fear gripped my heart, and I thought, "This might be it. This might be the end. This might be how I go down in the history books." My friend walking beside me leaned over and said, "Do you see that guy up there?" I said, "Yeah, bro." He whispered back, "This might be how we go down, bro!" I replied, "Yeah, man, this might be the end." It's funny to think about it now, but at that moment, paralyzing fear washed over me.

SCRIPTURES BEGAN TO FLOW LIKE A RIVER

The fear was so intense that I thought I would die standing there. At that moment, the phrase "sheep going to the slaughter" became very real! Then, the Holy Spirit spoke clearly to my heart. I remembered God's Word, and I began to quote the Bible: *"No weapon formed against [me] shall prosper"* (Isaiah 54:17). I spoke the words of Psalm 118:17 out loud: *"I shall not die, but live, and declare the works of the LORD."* Like water flowing down a river, Scripture verses began to flood my soul. *"A thousand fall at [my] side, and ten thousand at [my] right hand; but it shall not come near [me]"* (Psalm 91:7). *"We are more than conquerors through Him who loved us"* (Romans 8:37). *"The LORD is my helper; I will not fear. What can man do to me?"* (Hebrews 13:6).

I also remembered what David the psalmist wrote in Psalm 91:

> *He who dwells in the secret place of the Most High shall abide under the shadow of the Almighty. I will say of the Lord, "He is my refuge and my fortress; my God, in Him I will trust." Surely He shall deliver you from the snare of the fowler and from the perilous pestilence. He shall cover you with His feathers, and under His wings you shall take refuge; His truth shall be your shield and buckler. You shall not be afraid of the terror by night, nor of the arrow that flies by day, nor of the pestilence that walks in darkness, nor of the destruction that lays waste at noonday. A thousand may fall at your side, and ten thousand at your right hand; but it shall not come near you.* (Psalm 91:1–7)

Standing at the bottom of that stage, I placed my faith in what the Word said and not in my circumstances, and all the fear left me. Praise God, I have not felt fear like that in Pakistan ever since, and I have been there over twenty-four times since then.

I PLACED MY FAITH IN WHAT THE WORD SAID AND NOT IN MY CIRCUMSTANCES, AND ALL THE FEAR LEFT ME.

SPEAK THE WORD, READ THE WORD, QUOTE THE WORD, PRAY THE WORD

My friends, when you put your faith in the Word, there's power! Comfort, peace, and security appear when you know the Word of God will last forever and never fail. The Word is a firm foundation, tested and resting on solid ground. If you are going through a situation right now, I encourage you to read the Bible daily, search for the Scripture verses that are the promises for your situation, and stand on the Word, believing God for your miracle!

The Bible says that God's Word is a lamp to our feet and a light to our path. (See Psalm 119:105.) You can trust God's Word, for it is *more real than reality itself* because everything created came from God's Word—the birds of the air, the fish in the sea, the animals, trees, and all creation was created by God's Word. Remember, when God said, *"Let there be light"* (Genesis 1:3), light came into being. His Word spoke life into existence. His Word is more real than reality, so His Word can be trusted no matter how your situation may look.

If you're not getting into the Word daily, I recommend setting some time aside throughout your day to read and study the Bible. The average person spends over seven hours each day looking at a screen—TV, computer, cell phone. If you have time to watch TV or scroll on social media, you have more than enough time to read and meditate on God's Word. His Word is life and a firm foundation that you can build your life on. Wake up thirty minutes early every day and spend time with the God of creation, reading His Word, and watch your faith level grow. If you want strong faith, you need the Word in you. If you want to activate miracles in your life, you need the Word in you. You must never forget that *"faith comes by hearing, and hearing by the word of God"* (Romans 10:17).

If you don't know where to start reading, I highly recommend reading the gospel of John. It's an amazing book written by John, a disciple of Jesus. John had a profound revelation of God's love for him and for all humanity. You must get in the Word and study the Word for yourself. As you read, your faith will begin to build and rise. Start to declare the Word of God over your life and your circumstances, and watch your miracle come forth!

FOUR

A POWERFUL WITNESS
TO THE WORLD

"Oh that the Lord would saturate us through and through
with an undying zeal for the souls of men."[12]
—*Charles H. Spurgeon*

*"But you shall receive power when the Holy Spirit has come upon
you; and you shall be witnesses to Me in Jerusalem, and in all
Judea and Samaria, and to the end of the earth."*
—Acts 1:8

Jesus told His disciples that He had to leave them, but that He and
the Father were sending them a promise from heaven. *"Listen carefully:
I am sending the Promise of My Father [the Holy Spirit] upon you; but you*

---

12. Michael Brown, "Recovering the Priority of the Gospel," ChristianPost.com, https://
www.christianpost.com/voices/recovering-the-priority-of-the-gospel.html.

are to remain in the city [of Jerusalem] until you are clothed (fully equipped) with power from on high" (Luke 24:49 AMP). Why did Jesus tell them to remain in the city and wait? Because there was a supernatural power that they still needed before they could be His witnesses throughout the world. Jesus was saying, in effect, "Wait a minute; there is still something you need. There is more; there is so much more! Wait. Don't do anything until you receive the Father's promise of the Holy Spirit, until you receive power from on high. Don't leave Jerusalem. Don't start to talk among the people. Just wait together. I promise it's coming!"

Not long after, the promise came—a Holy Spirit baptism, a mighty rushing wind and tongues of fire.

When the Day of Pentecost had fully come, they were all with one accord in one place. And suddenly there came a sound from heaven, as of a rushing mighty wind, and it filled the whole house where they were sitting. Then there appeared to them divided tongues, as of fire, and one sat upon each of them. And they were all filled with the Holy Spirit and began to speak with other tongues, as the Spirit gave them utterance. (Acts 2:1–5)

WHY DID JESUS TELL THEM TO REMAIN IN THE CITY AND WAIT? BECAUSE THERE WAS A SUPERNATURAL POWER THAT THEY STILL NEEDED.

Why do you think this happened on the day of Pentecost? Pentecost (or the Day of First Fruits) is a Jewish feast first mentioned in Exodus, chapter 34, and generally celebrated on the fiftieth day after Passover. Jewish men who were able to make the pilgrimage would go to Jerusalem to celebrate. In Acts 2:5, Luke tells us there was a crowd of pilgrims in the city: *"And there were dwelling in Jerusalem Jews, devout men, from every nation under heaven."* That is why there were so many Jewish people from many other countries and languages in Jerusalem. This was the day that God chose to send His Holy Spirit in a baptism. So, Jesus not only told the disciples that the Holy Spirit would come upon them so that they could be His witnesses; He also sent the Spirit at a time when Jerusalem would be filled with a captive audience! Immediately after the disciples were filled with the Holy Spirit, they had both *the power* and *the opportunity* to be witnesses to Jewish men and women from every nation!

THE HOLY SPIRIT WITHIN

The moment we are born again, we receive the Holy Spirit. The Word of God says that He is the seal of our salvation. (See Ephesians 1:13.) The Holy Spirit came upon the apostles in this way after Jesus rose from the dead. When they were in a room together, Jesus breathed upon them and said that they should receive the Holy Spirit. *"Jesus said to them again, 'Peace to you! As the Father has sent Me, I also send you.' And when He had said this, He breathed on them, and said to them, 'Receive the Holy Spirit'"* (John 20:21–22). At that moment, they were sealed in their salvation. Yet, before Jesus ascended into heaven, He still said to them. "But wait in Jerusalem; I have more for you! I'm going to baptize you in power so that you can be witnesses of Me in Jerusalem and to the ends of the earth."

Thank You, Lord. Thank You for Your Word. Thank You for the Holy Spirit. Thank You for sending us the power from on high so that we can be witnesses to You throughout the earth. We can have faith in Your Word of promise!

After I was saved, all I wanted to do was read about Jesus. All I wanted to do was consume the Word of God. When I got to the book of Acts, I realized that God wants us to move in His power, to activate miracles by faith in His Word through the Holy Spirit. Shortly after, several Christians came to our Bible study and asked if anyone wanted to be filled with the Holy Spirit. We eagerly answered, "Yes!" God is a good Father. He will give the Holy Spirit to anyone who asks. *"If you then, being evil, know how to give good gifts to your children, how much more will your heavenly Father give the Holy Spirit to those who ask Him!"* (Luke 11:13).

God wants to fill you with the Holy Spirit so you can be a powerful witness to a lost and dying world. He also gives us the power of His Spirit to do greater things for His glory. Jesus promised us, *"Most assuredly, I say to you, he who believes in Me, the works that I do he will do also; and* **greater works** *than these he will do, because I go to My Father"* (John 14:12). If you want to receive the power of the Holy Spirit, ask Him to fill you now and receive the power in Jesus's name.

THE POWER TO TRANSFORM

We need a lot more of the Holy Spirit's power in these days. The word *power* in the New Testament is the Greek word *dunamis*, from which we get our word "dynamite."[13] It is the miraculous power of God. Explosive power. Not horsepower, not muscle power, but the power to perform miracles. *"'Not by might nor by power, but by My Spirit,' says the LORD of hosts"* (Zechariah 4:6). *"God anointed Jesus of Nazareth with the Holy Spirit and with power [dunamis], who went about doing good and healing all who were oppressed by the devil"* (Acts 10:38). God gives us the privilege and the authority to move in the power of the Spirit, as well.

It's amazing how the power of the Holy Spirit changed Peter in just a short time. Peter, who ran away in fear from the garden of Gethsemane. Peter, who would deny Jesus three times, just as He foretold. Peter, who even cursed a young servant girl in the courtyard before running scared from the scene. Yet on the morning of Pentecost, he was transformed

---

13. BibleHub.com, Greek #1411, *dunamis*, Strong's Greek: 1411. δύναμις (dunamis) -- (miraculous) power, might, strength (biblehub.com).

by the Holy Spirit and began preaching to the very same people that he had been so frightened of a few weeks earlier. Now, the Holy Spirit was moving through his life, and 3,000 people received salvation on that first day!

We need to shine stronger and brighter for Jesus in a world of increasing darkness. Jesus has commissioned us. *"And these signs will follow those who believe: In My name they will cast out demons; they will speak with new tongues...they will lay hands on the sick, and they will recover"* (Mark 16:17, 18).

> THIS WORLD NEEDS TO ENCOUNTER JESUS CHRIST AND HIS POWER TO SAVE, HEAL, AND DELIVER.

"GOD, THIS IS ALL I WANT TO DO!"

There are times when the Holy Spirit encourages us with prophetic words spoken over our lives. Of course, those words must line up with the Scriptures and be confirmed in other ways. The Lord has definitely used some prophetic words to encourage me along in my walk with Him.

A few years after Amanda and I were saved, a friend approached me and said, "Chris, you have a gift. I believe there is a gift from the Lord over your life—it's going to take you places you never imagined you would go." My first reaction was to think, "I'm just an average kind of guy. What would the Lord be calling me to do?" But in my heart, I wondered if the Lord was leading us to Bible college and perhaps into ministry after that. So, I applied and was accepted at Christ For the Nations Institute (CFNI) in Dallas, Texas, and Amanda and I moved across the country.

Students at CFNI were required to choose from a long list of Christian activities to be involved with outside the classroom. The one that jumped off the page to me was called "street evangelism." "That sounds exciting!" I thought. "I want to know how to tell people about Jesus!" The first time I went out evangelizing with a mentor, I was so nervous. I didn't want to talk to anybody! What would I say to lead someone to Jesus? What if I said the wrong thing? What if they asked questions to which I didn't have the answers?

Shortly after that, an opportunity arose to talk with a homeless man on a street in Dallas. While I was praying for him, the Holy Spirit spoke to me clearly about this man's life and gave me a prophetic word for him. I was nervous about sharing the prophetic word, so I started by asking the man, "Did you once follow God?"

He answered, "Yes, I did. I used to go to Bible studies as a teenager, but then I got mixed up with the wrong crowd and got into drugs."

"My friend," I replied, "God showed me while I was praying for you that you used to love the Lord, and you used to have a great relationship with Him, but you've gone astray. God says, 'It's time to come home.' It's time to turn from this lifestyle and turn back to Jesus. He died for your sins to set you free, and if you'll turn to Jesus today, He'll save you, forgive you, and give you a new life."

By this time the man was weeping uncontrollably. I wasn't sure what to do, since I had never led anyone to Jesus, but then I remembered how my pastor used to lead the call for salvation at the end of every church service. So, I asked this homeless man if he wanted to surrender his life to Christ, and he said yes. We prayed together right there on the streets of Dallas, and that man got right with God. Hallelujah!

"God, this is all I want to do," I prayed following that experience. "I just want to tell people about Jesus!" I began sharing Jesus at every opportunity, and I prayed, "Lord, I could never go back to the way I used to live. I'm all in, Jesus."

Just a few months later, a friend invited me to a Reinhard Bonnke conference in Dallas. I had never heard of Evangelist Bonnke, but he was one of the best-known evangelists in the world and had preached to tens of millions of people in Africa. Amanda and I attended the conference with our friends, and I was engrossed by Evangelist Bonnke's message and the teachings of his successor to the ministry, Daniel Kolenda. During one of the sessions, the friend who had invited me to the conference leaned over and said, "Chris, one day you're going to work for Daniel Kolenda." My reaction? "No way! That's never going to happen! Who am I?"

After the conference, I was considering my friend's words, and I prayed, "God, if You call me to do crusades, I'll go. I'll do whatever You want me to do. I'll go wherever You want me to go. Just show me if You're calling me to do crusades." Just fifteen minutes after I prayed, a friend messaged me online and said, "Chris, I had a dream about you last night. You were in a distant land, preaching the gospel to a crowd as far as the eye could see." "Bro," I wrote back, "you have no idea! I just prayed fifteen minutes ago and said, 'God, if You're calling me to do crusades, just show me. Just show me. I'll do whatever You want me to do.'" The Holy Spirit was moving in my life and giving me a clear call to evangelism.

"GOD, IF YOU CALL ME TO DO CRUSADES, I'LL GO. I'LL DO WHATEVER YOU WANT ME TO DO."

THE HOLY SPIRIT IS RIGHT ON TIME

As my time at school was drawing to a close, the Lord spoke to my heart, "After you graduate from Bible school, I'm going to connect you with an evangelist to learn from them before you start your own ministry." One morning, I had coffee with an evangelist whom I had met through the school; his name was Bernie Moore, and we are still friends to this day. After we shared our hearts for Jesus, Bernie said to me, "Chris, there is a calling on your life. Just this morning, I spoke with a friend of mine who is an evangelist and who is looking for a personal assistant. I just think you would be great for the job. His name is Daniel Kolenda."

My mouth dropped open; I was so overwhelmed! I was trying to act dignified, but inside I was praising God. I flew to Orlando to interview for the job and told Daniel that I believed the Lord wanted me to serve him in the ministry and to learn from him. Daniel answered, "I'll be sure to take time to train you to be an evangelist if I hire you." Shortly after, I learned that I'd gotten the job!

It was the beginning of an incredible adventure with Jesus—orchestrated by God and worked out in my life through His Holy Spirit. After serving and learning from Daniel Kolenda and Reinhard Bonnke for several years, in March of 2015, Amanda and I believed God was saying, "It's time to launch out." With Daniel and Reinhard's blessing, and with the Lord's guidance, we began to conduct our own crusades. God had prepared a way where there was no way—all for lost souls and His glory!

We started conducting crusades in India, Sri Lanka, and Pakistan with anywhere from 300-15,000 people in attendance. As the Lord blessed the work of our hands, the ministry began to flourish. Two years later, God opened a door for us to conduct open air crusades for tens of thousands of Pakistanis hungering for the message of Jesus. I love to see miracles, as God heals and delivers hurting people when we pray and believe God's Word in faith. But the desire of my heart is to see people saved, because that is the greatest miracle of all. The Bible says that when even one person comes to repentance, all of heaven rejoices! *"In the same way, I tell you, there is rejoicing in the presence of the angels of God over one sinner who repents"* (Luke 15:10 NIV). We rejoice that God has led us to be witnesses for His kingdom.

IS IT THE ATMOSPHERE OR OUR FAITH?

Preachers often say something like, "The presence of God is here, and now miracles are possible," or "The atmosphere is set for miracles," or "The glory of God is here, and now anything is possible." Honestly, I have made those kinds of statements myself. However, it is not true that miracles are more of a possibility when we feel God's presence or are under the "right" anointing or atmosphere. The miracles that occur as we minister do not happen because I felt God in a more supernatural way or had the perfect spiritual atmosphere. They happen because, knowing the promises of God found in His holy Word and having true faith to believe that those promises are still for today, we pray, trust, and expect the supernatural.

I don't recall Jesus having an anointed worship team following Him around with musical instruments to make miracles possible. The apostle Peter's shadow didn't heal people because he had Handel's "Hallelujah Chorus" being sung behind him. The apostle Paul didn't heal the sick, cast out demons, and even raise the dead just because he had the right atmosphere for miracles to be possible. Miracles happen for one reason: faith in the Word of God, by the power of the Holy Spirit.

Many people have asked me what I feel when I'm preaching to large crowds overseas. They want to know whether I feel a greater sense of the presence of God. They wonder about the spiritual atmosphere of my crusades. To be quite honest, most of the time, the atmosphere couldn't be worse when I preach the gospel overseas. It was not long ago that we saw the largest number of miracles at one of our crusades. It happened in Pakistan on a hot June night (the temperature reached 117 degrees during the day). At nine thirty, when I was handed the microphone to start preaching, the temperature was still a sweltering 107 degrees. Everyone in attendance was sweating profusely, including me. The crowd was fanning themselves with paper to cool down. As usual, some people were talking because it's almost impossible to quiet a crowd of over 100,000 people in an open field.

Thousands of people were still walking onto the field from the buses we had hired to transport them. Food vendors were trying to sell food on the street nearby. Police sirens were blaring in the background. We had to pause our meeting once so that the local mosque could have their time of prayer, since we didn't want to cause conflict with the local authorities or radicals in the area. Not only that, but a bug flew into my mouth while I was mid-sentence preaching the gospel. I paused to spit the bug out while my translator translated the first half of my sentence, and then I completed the sentence.

Truly, the atmosphere could not have been "worse" for a miracle. Yet it was in this place, under these seemingly impossible circumstances, that countless miracles started happening—not because we had the most anointed worship leaders, not because the atmosphere for miracles was just right, and not even because there was an anointing to heal that was present. It was because we had faith in the Word of God and the power of the Holy Spirit. We prayed with faith, expecting the Holy Spirit to show up, and He did. Praise God! Let me tell you about just one of the amazing miracles that took place that night.

IT WAS IN THIS PLACE, UNDER THESE SEEMINGLY IMPOSSIBLE CIRCUMSTANCES, THAT COUNTLESS MIRACLES STARTED HAPPENING.

A PARALYZED SON HEALED

After I preached the gospel, I began to pray for the sick, and the Holy Spirit started moving. We announced, "If you've been healed, please come forward to the side of the stage and testify to your miracle." Thousands of people came forward! I took testimonies for almost an hour from people who had been healed. After an hour, we noticed that the line for testimonies was still about a hundred yards long, and it was very late and very hot, so we decided to stop taking testimonies that night. The next day, we learned about a father and his three-year-old son who hadn't made it to the stage the previous evening.

The father was not a Christian; he was from a Muslim background and had seen an advertisement on Pakistani TV about our gospel campaign. Hearing that Jesus does miracles, he decided to travel seven hours with his crippled son to attend our meeting. That night, he heard me preach the gospel, give the altar call for salvation, and then pray for the sick. As soon as we started praying, his son, who had never been able to even move his legs, started moving them for the very first time and began to crawl. His father stood him up and watched as he began walking. He was totally healed! The next day, the father sent an offering into the ministry along with an email testimony of how God had healed his son. Most important, he told us that from that night forward, he, his wife, and his family would start serving Jesus Christ. Hallelujah!

THE HOLY SPIRIT DOESN'T CHANGE BY LOCATION

Many Christians tell me that miracles happen primarily on crusade fields or in churches in third-world countries rather than in the U.S., and then they give me one of several reasons why they have that belief. I have heard all the explanations as to why more miracles happen overseas than in America, and my response to every one of them is the same: the same Holy Spirit who does miracles at crusades in Pakistan, Africa, and elsewhere is right here with us in America, and He can heal in America just as easily as He can in Africa or Pakistan. The Holy Spirit doesn't change according to location, and His power is not determined by zip code or country codes. God's power is within all who call upon His name and have been baptized in the power of the Holy Spirit, according to Luke 24:49 and Acts 1:8.

The reason most people don't see miracles happening in churches in the U.S. has nothing to do with location. It has nothing to do with how desperate people are overseas, and it has nothing to do with how hungry people are to receive miracles. I have seen God do mighty miracles in all these circumstances. The reason miracles don't happen as much in the U.S. is that most American preachers don't preach about healing; they don't pray for the sick and expect miracles to happen. Too many pastors are afraid of what their congregation or their financial supporters will think if they preach about faith and healing.

I'll say it again: The power for miracles is in the belief and the declaration of God's Word and by the power of the Holy Spirit. His Word never changes. His Word is everywhere the truth is, and it's the truth that sets people free. (See John 8:32.) His Word is where faith is. Faith does not come by need, and faith does not come by location or desperation. Faith comes in one way: hearing and trusting in the Word of God! I'm not ashamed of the gospel. I'm not ashamed of preaching something that might offend some people. I'm not afraid of preaching what might not make sense in the natural to someone who doesn't understand or believe God's Word.

THE POWER FOR MIRACLES IS IN THE BELIEF AND THE DECLARATION OF GOD'S WORD AND BY THE POWER OF THE HOLY SPIRIT.

A MIRACLE IN THE UNITED STATES

A few years ago, I was speaking at a church in Jacksonville, Florida, where I frequently preach. That Sunday morning, I shared the gospel and talked about God's desire to heal, and then I began praying for the sick. While I was at the altar laying hands on people, a twenty-something-year-old woman stopped me and told me she had recently been in a major car accident. Her arm was so severely broken from the accident that the doctors used metal rods and bolts to piece her entire arm back together. As a result, she experienced constant throbbing pain, and she had lost a lot of mobility in that arm.

I laid hands on her and prayed for her to be completely healed in Jesus's name. God touched her, and she was instantly and completely healed. Not only did all the pain leave her body, but full mobility was restored to her arm. I don't know whether God took the metal out of her body or if He just made it elastic, but I do know that she was supernaturally healed. Since then, we have been back to that church many times, and I always look for the young woman God healed from that car accident. I ask her how she's doing, and every time she tells me, "I'm still completely healed in Jesus's name!" Hallelujah!

MIRACLE OF STOPPING THE RAIN IN INDIA

There are always amazing testimonies when you speak the Word in faith by the power of the Holy Spirit. On one of the first nights of a crusade in India, I was sharing the gospel with several thousand people in attendance. As soon as I received the microphone to start preaching, massive drops of rain started falling, and we knew we were about to experience a downpour. I opened my mouth to speak, and the huge raindrops started coming down with greater intensity. At that moment, I turned to the sky and declared, "In the mighty name of Jesus, I command this rain to stop right now, in Jesus's name! Amen." When I said "Amen," the rain stopped completely. The crowd let out a collective gasp when they realized what had happened. I proceeded to preach the gospel under dry skies. Then, as soon as I started to give the altar call for salvation, it seemed as if the enemy wanted to stop our crusade. Large raindrops started falling again, this time more quickly. You could tell that it was about to start pouring on all of us.

I resisted the enemy again by lifting my eyes to heaven and declaring, "In the name of Jesus, I command all this rain to stop now!" Then I added, "Don't return again, in Jesus's name. Amen!" Once again, as soon as I said "Amen," the rain immediately stopped. You could hear people gasping even more loudly at the miracle they had just experienced. I made the call for salvation, and that night it was as if everyone wanted to get saved. Thousands of people responded to the altar call to receive Jesus. It's amazing how God will use miracles to attract people to the gospel. Throughout the New Testament, we see this happening in the life and ministry of Jesus and His disciples. Jesus often healed people, cast out demons, used prophetic words, and even raised the dead to life in order to confirm His identity and the message He preached. (See, for example, John 11:1–40; Acts 2:22.)

The story of rain miraculously stopping during the crusade in India began spreading throughout the surrounding villages. The people in this remote part of India were talking about the man who preaches and commands the rain to stop in Jesus's name. By the end of the week, the crowd had nearly doubled, and thousands received Jesus as their Lord and Savior, in part because of having witnessed the supernatural. The local pastors were excited because it didn't rain for the rest of that weeklong crusade. They joked that I had not only prayed for the rain to stop for the crusade but also that it would not come back again. Even though the weather forecasters called for a hundred percent chance of rain daily, God stopped the rain that week, and we had a mighty crusade.

HIS POWER WORKING THROUGH US

Yes, the power of the Holy Spirit resides within me. Yes, God's Word tells me, "You heal the sick; you cast out demons." But it's not my power that heals the sick. It's not my power that sets captives free. It's not my power that commands the rain to stop. It is His power at work through me. However, God still wants me to step out in faith and lay hands on the sick, cast out the enemy, and set captives free. As Reinhard Bonnke used to say, "God works with workers. He doesn't sit with sitters." I tell people, "I'm just an evangelist who preaches the gospel and prays for the sick, and Jesus does the saving, and He does the healing, and He does the baptism of the Holy Spirit." I also say to others, "Listen. I believe that this gospel is so true that God is willing to confirm the message that I preach with miracles, signs, and wonders, according to Mark 16."

My friends, God wants one thing: for people to know Him and His Son, Jesus Christ, the Savior of the world. Jesus came for one primary purpose—to seek and to save the lost (See Luke 19:10)—and He will give you power through His Holy Spirit to step out of the natural into the supernatural to show the world that Jesus Christ is Lord.

IT'S NOT MY POWER THAT SETS CAPTIVES FREE. IT IS HIS POWER AT WORK THROUGH ME.

FIVE

FAITH IS SPELLED
T-R-U-S-T

"True faith rests upon the character of God and
asks no further proof than the moral perfections of the One
who cannot lie."[14]
—*A. W. Tozer*

*"Trust in the Lord with all your heart and lean not on your own
understanding; in all your ways acknowledge Him,
and He shall direct your paths."*
—Proverbs 3:5–6

Can you imagine a tightrope stretching over a quarter of a mile and
spanning the breadth of Niagara Falls? The thundering sound of the

---

14. GoodReads.com, "A. W. Tozer Quotes," https://www.goodreads.com/author/
quotes/1082290.A_W_Tozer.

pounding water drowning out all other sounds as you watch a man step onto a tightrope and walk across? You may have heard the story of Charles Blondin, the famous French acrobat who crossed over Niagara Falls on a tightrope many times in the 1850s and 1860s. On June 30, 1859, Blondin stunned the world by walking across Niagara Falls for the first time. The story is a perfect illustration of the difference between casual belief and true faith.

Blondin's tightrope was suspended across the 1100-foot gorge between Canada and the United States above the raging waters; he had no harness or safety net. Reports say that over 100,000 people gathered to watch him walk across the Falls for the first time. Over the years, Blondin crossed Niagara Falls multiple times, doing many theatrical variations. He went across blindfolded. He went across on stilts, in a sack, and carrying a man on his back. At one time, he even pushed a wheelbarrow. The wheelbarrow story is the greatest of all.[15]

Blondin's rope was stretched from one side of Niagara Falls to the other. He built a billboard-sized-advertisement to draw a large crowd that would watch him complete this death-defying act. Before he stepped onto the tightrope, he turned and asked the crowd, "How many of you think I can walk across Niagara Falls?" Nobody said a word. So, he turned back and began taking his first steps, walking out on the tightrope over Niagara Falls. Soon, he had crossed over to the other side of the Falls, turned around, and journeyed back to where he had begun.

Thousands celebrated his successful walk across Niagara Falls. Blondin called out to the crowd a second time, "How many of you think I can take a wheelbarrow across Niagara Falls and come back?" This time they clapped and cheered, shouting, "We believe you can do it!" So, he grabbed a wheelbarrow and crossed the tightrope for a second time. After completing the wheelbarrow act to great applause, Blondin asked

15. Tom Steele, "Faith That Works," https://sermons.logos.com/sermons/939044-5.-faith-that-works.

a new question: "Now, how many of you believe I can put a person in this wheelbarrow and walk out across Niagara Falls?" They were cheering and chanting, "Yes, we believe you can do it!" "Great!" he responded. "Do I have any volunteers?" The crowd quickly went silent.

What a great example of the wide gap between superficially *believing* and having *faith*. While the people believed Blondin could carry someone across the Falls in a wheelbarrow, they did not have enough faith in him to get into the wheelbarrow and make the trip. You see, it's easy to say we have faith, but true faith is getting into God's wheelbarrow and trusting that even through life's difficulties, He will get us safely to the other side. We can trust that God will protect us and watch over us. No matter what the circumstances look like, we can trust in Jesus! The next time you are questioning, just remember that faith is getting into God's wheelbarrow and trusting Him completely.

TRUST IN THE LORD WITH ALL YOUR HEART

To have true faith, we must realize that faith is spelled T-R-U-S-T. The Bible says that we are to *"trust in the Lord **with all** [our] heart"* (Proverbs 3:5). Trust is based on faith in a God who is trustworthy. We trust God because we believe that He is faithful; we have confidence that He will do what He has promised. If you trust God's Word, you have faith in His Word because they are synonymous. Faith requires trust.

Faith is not merely a superficial belief or an intellectual understanding. Faith is not just believing that something is true. The Bible says that even demons believe God exists—and they tremble. (See James 2:19.) Genuine faith is a willingness to wholeheartedly trust, and it has God as its object. It means believing we are reconciled to God through His Son Jesus Christ, surrendering our lives to Him, and trusting in the absolute truth of His Word. Dr. John Phillips, a British/Canadian Bible teacher and author of the *John Phillips Commentaries*, explains,

"Faith gives substance to the unseen realities. The believer hopes in these things and proves their reality in his personal experience by faith. Faith is a kind of spiritual 'sixth sense' that enables the believer to take a firm hold upon the unseen world and bring it into the realm of experience."[16] Trust and faith merge, making it possible to accomplish the impossible. If we have great faith, we must trust the Lord with our whole heart and not lean on our own understanding.

*TRUST IS BASED ON FAITH IN A GOD
WHO IS TRUSTWORTHY.*

"THE JUST SHALL LIVE BY FAITH"

One single Old Testament verse—*"But the just shall live by his faith"* (Habakkuk 2:4), which is repeated in the New Testament—has done more to revolutionize our faith in Jesus Christ than almost any other. This verse lit a fire in the heart of Martin Luther and ignited the Protestant Reformation 500 years ago. It also opened Augustine's eyes in the fourth century AD and established him as a mighty man of faith in the early church. It is still striking fire in countless hearts today.

Three different New Testament books quote Habakkuk's verse on the just living by faith—Romans 1:17, Galatians 3:11, and Hebrews 10:8. In addition to this verse, the book of Hebrews has a great deal to say about the history and power of faith in God. Faith is mentioned thirty-one times in Hebrews, twenty-three times in chapter eleven alone. Let's look at a few of those faith verses.

---

16. Reference needed. I couldn't locate one online.

"*For indeed the gospel was preached to us as well as to them; but the word which they heard did not profit them, **not being mixed with faith** in those who heard it*" (Hebrews 4:2). The focus of the fourth chapter of Hebrews is "entering God's rest," but the Israelites could not enter the presence and rest of God because they had an unclean mixture of fear and faith.

"*But without faith it is impossible to please Him, for he who comes to God must believe that He is, and that He is a rewarder of those who diligently seek Him*" (Hebrews 11:6). By your faith, you give pleasure to God. Without faith, you are unable to trust God and therefore cannot please Him. God cannot be pleased with those who have no confidence in Him, who doubt the truth of His Word, who do not trust in His ways.

"*Looking unto Jesus, the author and finisher of our faith, who for the joy that was set before Him endured the cross, despising the shame, and has sat down at the right hand of the throne of God*" (Hebrews 12:2). Jesus is the Author and the Finisher of our faith. Fixing our eyes on Jesus means directing our attention to Him without distraction. We look to Jesus, the perfector, finisher, originator, and completer of our faith. We look to the Word of God because we already understand that Jesus *is* the Word of God. (See John 1:1.)

Over fifteen faith heroes are mentioned in the "Faith Hall of Fame," which is Hebrews, chapter 11; but Abraham and Moses are the only two heroes who are mentioned twice. "*By faith Abraham obeyed when he was called to go out to the place which he would receive as an inheritance. And he went out, not knowing where he was going*" (Hebrews 11:8). "*By faith Abraham, when he was tested, offered up Isaac, and he who had received the promises offered up his only begotten son,…concluding that God was able to raise him up, even from the dead…*" (Hebrews 11:17, 19). Both times, *by faith,* Abraham denied himself and chose obedience to God, obeying the Father's will. Yes, faith enables us to *obtain the promises* of God, but faith also enables us to *obey the commands* of God.

Faith gives us the strength to obey when obedience is costly or seems unreasonable to the natural mind.

FAITH ENABLES US TO OBTAIN THE PROMISES OF GOD, BUT FAITH ALSO ENABLES US TO OBEY THE COMMANDS OF GOD.

HOW TO ACTIVATE YOUR FAITH

When you receive a new debit or credit card, you cannot use it until it is activated. When an automobile factory builds a car, it belongs to the dealership that bought it until you, the customer, make the purchase. Once it belongs to you, you first must activate your insurance and then activate the keys before you drive away. In the same way, if you have a dream or a call on your life, it won't happen until you activate it, making it a reality through action.

Having faith without walking it out is not enough. God will never bring about the call on your life until your faith is activated. You will never walk in *supernatural faith without limits* unless you move forward in faith. James 2:26 admonishes us, *"For as the body without the spirit is dead, so faith without works is dead also."* James uses the example of Abraham's faith *"working together with his works"* when he offered Isaac on the altar. (See James 2:21–22.) God acts according to your faith. When you have a burning desire to fulfill God's will, and you step out speaking the Word as if you already have it, it will activate the faith to fulfill it.

In Luke 9:1–2, Jesus understood the importance of activating His disciples' faith by giving them power and authority over demons and diseases, then sending them out to preach and heal the people, without the ability to lean on Him. Jesus sent the disciples out, but the miraculous wasn't activated until they actually left Jesus and began praying for the sick and demon possessed. *"So, they departed and went through the towns, preaching the gospel and healing everywhere"* (Luke 9:6).

When the Word of God is spoken, it is activated flawlessly, performs with power, and penetrates your every thought. The Bible tells us, *"The word of God is alive and **active** [energes]"* (Hebrews 4:12 NIV). The Greek word *energes* means active (activated), operative, effectual, and powerful.[17] In Romans 5:1–2, Paul declares, *"Therefore, having been justified by faith, we have peace with God through our Lord Jesus Christ, through whom also we have **access by faith** into this grace in which we stand, and rejoice in hope of the glory of God."* We have access by faith through Jesus Christ.

Paul spoke to the Corinthian church about the effective, activating power of God, saying, *"But I will tarry in Ephesus until Pentecost. For a **great and effective door** has opened to me, and there are many adversaries"* (1 Corinthians 16:8–9). Paul chose to stay in Ephesus, despite the adversaries, because something was activated in the supernatural: a great and *effective* (activated) door had opened to him. It took the supernatural to activate the desire Paul had for Ephesus. An effective door is an activated door, and an activated door by faith opens a supernatural life *without limits.* Paul also initiated something powerful in Philemon's life when he prayed that the disciple's faith would be *effective* (activated) for God's purposes in his life: *"I pray that the sharing of your faith **may become effective** and powerful because of your accurate knowledge of every good thing which is ours in Christ"* (Philemon 6 AMP).

---

17. Blue Letter Bible, https://www.blueletterbible.org/lexicon/g1756/kjv/tr/0-1/.

When faith is activated, the lost come to Christ, divine healing happens, deep needs are fulfilled, and people are lifted above the burdens and storms of their lives. If you are going to stand in faith, you must realize that faith doesn't start when a miracle happens; faith starts the moment you trust in the One who performs miracles. You don't have faith for a miracle *after* the miracle; you have faith *before* you ever see the miracle fulfilled.

> YOU DON'T HAVE FAITH FOR A MIRACLE AFTER THE MIRACLE; YOU HAVE FAITH BEFORE YOU EVER SEE THE MIRACLE FULFILLED.

THE HEALING POWER OF JESUS

A couple of years ago, I was preaching at a church in Houston, Texas. At the end of the service, I prayed for the sick as I often do, and God touched a man who was eighty-three years old and had come to the church using a walker. He had had a stroke a few years earlier, leaving the right side of his body crippled so that he only had partial mobility in his right leg. He would use his walker to take one step with his good leg and drag the other leg behind him; he couldn't walk without it.

I gave a short message on healing from God's Word and then started to pray. While praying over the congregation, I said something I had never said before: "You're never too old to get your healing, and you are never too young to get your healing. Healing doesn't have age restrictions. Now be healed, in Jesus's name." I believe it was a prophetic word from God for this elderly man. At that moment, faith started to rise in his spirit. Later he told me that he said to himself, "Yes! I'm not too old to get healed. God's Word is true no matter my age." His faith grew stronger as I encouraged the crowd, "Now, do something you couldn't do before. If you can't walk, start walking. If you can't see, start looking. If you can't bend over, then bend over and see how God has healed you."

Without hesitating, the elderly man pushed his walker to the side and started walking without it. He walked faster and faster across the church's altar, tears streaming down his face as he said, "I'm not going back. I'm not going back to thinking that way again. I'm not too old for my healing. I've got my healing now, in Jesus's name!" At that moment, he was completely healed and gave Jesus all the glory. Praise God, he had activated his faith by walking it out in Jesus's name!

The next day, the pastor of the church sent me a text that read, "Do you remember the older man who was healed yesterday? He called me today and said he woke up without his hearing aids in his ears, and he could hear perfectly without them!" Praise God! Jesus heals! His Word is true and eternal! As it says in Mark 16:18, *"They will lay hands on the sick, and they shall recover."*

ACTIVATING FAITH FOR MIRACLES

To effectively activate your faith for the supernatural, you must know the depths of God's reality and power, as well as His promises and will for you. When you act upon God's Word, you will activate His power and strength. In 1 Samuel, chapter 30, we read that while they were away in battle, David's family and the families of his warriors were kidnapped by the Amalekites at Ziglak. David was distraught by this loss and also because his own soldiers were threatening to stone him. However, when he activated his faith, he became strengthened in the Lord his God. *"Now David was greatly distressed, for the people spoke of stoning him, because the soul of all the people was grieved, every man for his sons and his daughters. But David strengthened himself in the* Lord *his God"* (1 Samuel 30:6). Refreshed in faith, David led his army to overcome the enemy and successfully rescue all their families. This is activated faith!

Corrie ten Boom had a famous saying: "If you have the faith, God has the power!" You activate your faith by hearing, speaking, and trusting the powerful Word of God. The Word you feed on determines the direction of your faith because, as we have said, *"Faith comes by hearing, and hearing by the word of God"* (Romans 10:17). So, faith must find expression in hearing God's Word.

The apostle Peter didn't know what would happen when he climbed out of that boat and stepped on the water. His faith was activated the moment he stepped out of the boat, not after he walked on the water. In the same way, faith starts when you trust and believe and say, "Jesus, I believe Your Word, and I believe You can! I believe that You can protect me because Your Word says so; I believe that You can heal me because Your Word say so; and I believe that You can move in my life no matter what the situation is because Your Word declares it." The Word you believe activates your faith into action. It's faith, together with works—good works done in obedience to God's commandments are the fruit and evidence of genuine, activated faith. In answering God's call to evangelize, I obeyed Him and activated my faith in miracles in so many ways.

GOOD WORKS DONE IN OBEDIENCE TO GOD'S COMMANDMENTS ARE THE FRUIT AND EVIDENCE OF GENUINE, ACTIVATED FAITH.

HEALED OF PARKINSON'S DISEASE

As I've shared, I was raised in a small town in central Minnesota. The town's population is only 1700, and "everybody knows everybody." In the spring of 2021, my mom, Virginia Mikkelson, a wonderful woman of faith, passed away after a four-year battle with cancer at the age of seventy-four. She and my dad laid a foundation of trust in Jesus in my life, even though I ran from it in my rebellious years. Although we didn't see my mom's healing on the earth, we know she is healed and whole in heaven with Jesus today.

My mom's funeral was planned for Saturday, May 8, 2021. In our town, it is customary to have a "wake" the night before so the townspeople can pay their last respects to the family. That Friday night, as I stood at the altar beside my father, sister, and brother in the small country Lutheran church where I grew up, hundreds of people stood in line, ready to offer their support and condolences.

During the evening, an older man approached me; a friend of my father that I had known since I was a boy. (For privacy, we will call him Ole). Ole had several children with whom I had grown up playing and celebrating birthday parties. He doesn't have a Pentecostal or charismatic background, but he is a lover of Jesus who attends a small country church, sings in the all-men's choir with my dad, and spends weekends volunteering for the Gideons by handing out Bibles. He didn't look very well that night; he walked hunched over and struggled to stand even with his cane. When I asked him what had happened, he tried to talk but was having difficulty speaking. His wife explained that Ole had contracted Parkinson's disease fifteen years earlier, and he was getting worse and worse. His doctors had prescribed fifteen pills daily for his condition, but nothing was helping.

My heart broke for Ole, and, at that moment, the words that came tumbling out of my mouth shocked even me. I asked him,

"Can I pray for you?" Now, normally, such a request would not have shocked me; I always pray for the sick, and we see God do many miracles. But this didn't seem like the "right" time to pray for the sick. Remember, too often, people expect a certain kind of atmosphere when healings will occur. There wasn't a choir behind me singing the "Hallelujah Chorus." It wasn't altar time at the end of a powerful Sunday sermon. But none of that matters when you know God and His Word.

Ole replied immediately, "Sure! I can always use prayer." I laid my hand on his shoulder and said, "Father, I come to You in the name of Jesus. Be healed of Parkinson's disease right now, in Jesus's name! Amen." By this time, the line had backed up behind us, but we both knew that God had a purpose in that prayer time.

"YOU'VE GOT TO SHOW SOME FAITH"

Once Ole stepped outside the church, in his spirit he heard God say, "Now, you've got to show some faith." At first, he questioned what it meant to show faith, and then in his heart he knew—he needed to start slowly reducing his medication from fifteen tablets to one less each day. He didn't do this because I told him to, and I'm not telling you to do this if you're on medication. Ole did it because he heard the voice of God. Faith doesn't come from the evangelist or the pastor; the Bible says that faith comes by hearing God's voice.

The next day Ole secretly reduced his medicine from fifteen to fourteen pills and immediately started feeling better. Over the next fourteen days, he weaned himself off all medication and hasn't looked back. He testified that all his symptoms of Parkinson's disease were totally gone! He couldn't wait to hear his doctors confirm what God already had done. On two separate occasions, he sent me the testimonies of what his specialists said during his checkups once he was off all medication. The first specialist appointment was three months after I prayed for him.

Here is the text: "Greetings, Chris and Amanda! An update from my appointment with my neurologist at Sanford Clinic, Fargo, on Tuesday, August 17, 2021. After going through the usual test procedures for analysis with quite different results from the past, the doctor paused and said, 'I agree, Ole; it is a miracle'!" Praise God!

His second specialist also confirmed the results. I received a text again a month later: "Happy Labor Day weekend, Pastor and Mrs. Mikkelson! Almost four months since we prayed together. An update: Last Thursday, I had an appointment at Sanford Hospital, Fargo, for a complex brain scan—NM BRAIN SPECT WITH DATSCAN. (Done to see if I still have PD symptoms.) Comments from the doctor, 'Your DaTscan was negative, indicating that you do NOT have Parkinson's disease.' Praise God! I've been touched by the Master's hand!" Hallelujah!

Our God still heals today, and we can *trust* Him! Faith is trusting what we know to be true about the character of God. If you know His Word and character, you can take a position of faith and see the supernatural manifest in your life. Ole might not be from a Pentecostal church, but he took a position of faith. He activated his faith by obeying God's voice to ease off his medication, and he trusted God and His Word. He is still healed today because of it.

FAITH DOESN'T COME FROM THE EVANGELIST OR THE PASTOR; THE BIBLE SAYS THAT FAITH COMES BY HEARING GOD'S VOICE.

AN INTERESTING ILLUSTRATION OF ACTIVATED FAITH

Most of us are familiar with the American Revolution, also known as the War of Independence. The best-known date from that time period is July 4, 1776, when the United States declared independence from Great Britain. We commemorate the Fourth of July annually with picnics, fireworks, and other festive celebrations of our nation's freedom.

However, July 4, 1776, did not mark the official date of our nation's independence. The Revolutionary War did not end for another seven *years* after the Declaration of Independence was signed. The details are included in the Treaty of Paris, signed by Benjamin Franklin, John Adams, and John Jay at the Hotel d'York in Paris, finalized on September 3, 1783, and ratified by the Continental Congress on January 14, 1784.

So, why don't we celebrate our independence on September 3rd? Why do we consider July 4th to be the date when our nation's freedom began? It is because July 4, 1776, is the date when our forefathers signed the Declaration of Independence with the faith that their country would overcome England. It is the date we celebrate because it was the day that America declared her freedom!

FAITH DOESN'T COME AFTER YOU WIN THE WAR, JUST AS FAITH DOESN'T COME AFTER YOU RECEIVE THE MIRACLE.

Faith doesn't come after you win the war, just as faith doesn't come after you receive the miracle. Faith starts the moment you first trust and believe! America's forefathers didn't have proof that they would win their independence. Yet, they wrote and signed the Declaration of Independence to declare that America was free. It was an act of faith to declare independence even though they had not yet seen the victory. Praise God, they had the conviction to proclaim that it was already done!

You can choose today to make your own declarations. You can declare today that you are free, that you are healed, that you will overcome, that your family will be saved, that your marriage will be blessed, and that you will prosper in every area of life. Whatever your situation, you can stand in faith and declare that it's already finished *according to the Word of God*. You can say, "You know what, devil? I don't care what the circumstances are; I'm trusting God. I will pursue God, live for Him all my days, and see the miraculous in my life."

Today, purpose to do whatever He's called you to do. Declare that you are going to believe and trust God. Faith starts the moment you first believe. Whatever you trust God for, your purpose today is to believe Him. Make your declarations and watch God transform your situation and your life!

SIX

HAVE FAITH, NOT FEAR

"Danger is real, but fear is a choice."[18]
—*Pastor Khalid Naz*

"Fear not, for I am with you; be not dismayed, for I am your God."
—Isaiah 41:10

W hat is this thing called fear? God created our brains to be so incredibly complex that they respond to danger even before we have processed the threat we face. Fear starts with a stimulus that triggers chemicals in the brain that signal your heart, blood, and muscles to get ready for quick action. This "fight or flight" response is God's protection for us from danger. But did you know that God never intended for you to live in a state of fear? The Bible says, *"Do not fear,"* which means God

---

18. Shawn Williams, "World Harvest Outreach Pakistan Update!" February 11, 2015, Warrior Nations International Ministries, https://warriornations.org/evangelism/world-harvest-outreach-pakistan-update/.

never intended anxiety or distress to rule our lives or take root in our hearts. God never meant for us to be people of fear but people of faith. He never wanted us to be people of worry but people of peace.

Fear is one of Satan's most destructive tools. He uses it to blind us from seeing what God calls us to do. Fear steals our faith; where there is fear, there is no faith because fear and faith cannot coexist. Throughout life, we will face distressing situations that could cause us to fear, but God assures us that we can know His calming peace through every situation. As the apostle Paul puts it, "*Do not be anxious about anything, but in every situation, by prayer and petition, with thanksgiving, present your requests to God. And **the peace of God**, which transcends all understanding, will guard your hearts and your minds in Christ Jesus*" (Philippians 4:6–7 NIV).

The Bible contains 365 phrases or commands concerning fear, such as, "Do not fear," "Do not be afraid," and "Fear not." "Fear not," because too many people live in a world full of fear and anxiety. In the Old Testament, David discovered an antidote to fear, which he described as follows: "*I sought the LORD, and He heard me, and delivered me from all my fears*" (Psalm 34:4). David found his strength in the Lord and rejected all elements of fear. Many verses from the Psalms capture his confidence including the following: "*Though an army may encamp against me, my heart shall not fear; though war may rise against me, in this I will be confident*" (Psalm 27:3). "*He shall cover you with His feathers, and under His wings you shall take refuge; His truth shall be your shield and buckler. You shall not be afraid of the terror by night, nor of the arrow that flies by day*" (Psalm 91:5–6).

The Bible reminds us that we can trust God as our good Father. "*I will be a Father to you, and you shall be My sons and daughters, says the LORD Almighty*" (2 Corinthians 6:18). He will fight for us and cover us and protect us. He will calm the storms in our minds and hearts, but He asks that we turn our eyes away from our fears to Him. If we take our faith seriously, we must listen to the clues that can trigger fear. Jesus often talked about overcoming fear, worry, and anxiety because He didn't want us to lose sight of what was most important in life.

Jesus had no fear, for it had no power over Him, and nothing surprised or unsettled Him. Even in the garden of Gethsemane, even when His sweat became drops of blood, Jesus poured out His heart to the Father and declared His commitment to trust God. Throughout His life on earth, Jesus walked with determination to Calvary without fearing men or circumstances. Why? Because He knew the character of God the Father. Before ascending to heaven, Jesus left this word for all of us to cure our fears: *"Peace I leave with you; my peace I give you. I do not give to you as the world gives. Do not let your hearts be troubled and do not be afraid"* (John 14:27 NIV).

> *JESUS HAD NO FEAR, FOR IT HAD NO POWER OVER HIM, AND NOTHING SURPRISED OR UNSETTLED HIM.*

"FEAR NOT, FOR I AM WITH YOU"

Charles Spurgeon was a fiery British preacher, pastor, and author of the nineteenth century. On April 9, 1870, at the Metropolitan Tabernacle in London, Spurgeon preached a sermon entitled "Away with Fear." He spoke from Isaiah 41:10, which reads, *"**Fear not**, for I am with you; be not dismayed, for I am your God. I will strengthen you, yes, I will help you, I will uphold you with My righteous right hand."* Spurgeon addressed three critical areas about fear: the *disease* of fear, the *command* not to fear, and God's *promise* to help us overcome fear.[19]

The disease of fear: "This disease of fear came into man's heart with sin," Spurgeon said. "Adam never was afraid of his God till he had broken his commands....It is sin, consciousness of sin, that 'makes cowards of us all.'"

We shouldn't let sin cause us to fear. If we repent of sin, it will eliminate fear and lead us to faith.

The command not to fear: God commands us often with the words, *"Fear not; be not dismayed."* That morning, Spurgeon asked this question: "Is not unbelief a robbery of God, a treason felony against him? If I were in conversation with any one of you, and you should say to me, 'Sir, I cannot believe you,' nothing you could say would sting me more."

When we ignore God's command to fear not, we are telling Him that we don't believe Him or trust His words!

God's promise to overcome fear: Finally, God promises to help us overcome fear and dismay according to His will. Spurgeon pointed out that in all five lines of Isaiah 41:10, God uses both the words *you* and *I* in a pledge to be our help and our strength: "Fear not, for *I* am with *you*! Be not dismayed, for *I* am *your* God! *I* will strengthen *you*! Yes, *I* will help *you*! *I* will uphold *you* with My righteous right hand." Spurgeon ended his sermon with these words: "Here you have angels' food; nay, the very bread of life itself lies within these choice words. The only fear I have is lest you should miss them through unbelief. 'O taste and see that the Lord is good.'"

Don't miss the power of God's Word to uphold you and help you conquer fear in your life!

---

19. Charles Haddon Spurgeon, "Away with Fear," April 9, 1970, The Spurgeon Center for Biblical Preaching at Midwestern Seminary, https://www.spurgeon.org/resource-library/ sermons/away-with-fear/#flipbook/.

OVERCOMING FEAR IN PAKISTAN DURING
THE COVID-19 PANDEMIC

In September 2020, six months into the Covid-19 pandemic, I received a phone call from our Pakistan crusade director informing me that our crusade permits—which had been pending for six months due to Covid restrictions—had just been approved. We would be able to conduct the crusade just two months later, in November 2020. I was thrilled knowing that we could go back to the people who needed the good news of Jesus Christ!

In the Spirit, I knew that God had called us to do this crusade. He spoke to me clearly about going, but still fear wanted to stop us. The thought of flying in the middle of a worldwide pandemic plagued our thoughts. "What's it going to be like traveling during Covid?" we thought. "What about getting tested? What if the government tries to shut us down and we lose tens of thousands of dollars when we get there?"

A few evangelical leaders warned us, "I wouldn't go to Pakistan right now." Other people, including some pastors, thought it was reckless to conduct a crusade with so many people gathered in one place at the height of Covid. But for me, it was a simple decision. If we didn't go, how many thousands, maybe tens of thousands of people, would get sick, die, and spend an eternity in hell separated from God?

That is why evangelism is essential, crusades are essential, and the church is essential, in Jesus's name. It is the call on my life to bring the good news of Jesus to a lost world. If we don't go, many will not know, and it's up to us as Christians to give everyone the opportunity to receive Jesus. It might have seemed reckless to some, but the Lord spoke to me very clearly, and we stepped out in faith—despite fear's attempts to hold us back.

Here's the truth: fear paralyzes, but faith energizes; fear terrorizes, but faith harmonizes; fear minimizes, but faith maximizes! When fear wants to grip your mind, you can choose faith and expect to overcome it, in Jesus's name.

> *FEAR PARALYZES, BUT FAITH ENERGIZES; FEAR TERRORIZES, BUT FAITH HARMONIZES; FEAR MINIMIZES, BUT FAITH MAXIMIZES!*

Of course, there is often a battle of faith to overcome fear! One of our biggest fears was getting a Covid test in Pakistan before flying back to the U.S. Several Christian friends told us that when they were tested in Pakistan, it was a very painful experience. The testing stick was just a plastic instrument with no cotton swab at the end of it. They said it was "shoved several inches up their nose toward their brain" to get a result. One Pakistani friend admitted his nose hurt for weeks after getting tested this way. My reaction to all of this was, "They did what!?"

It all turned out to be true, and now fear started creeping in. At that moment, I could have listened to my fear, but I said, "No, I'm going to trust the Lord." I started making statements of faith to myself and my wife, saying, "We're going to be fine. God will protect us. He will make a way where there seems to be no way."

ARRIVING IN PAKISTAN

Once we arrived in Pakistan, our airline sent us a list of clinics where we could get tested for our flight home. We had to use one of their four "approved" clinics and no other. I sent the list to our director's wife to book our exam; to my horror, she had never heard of any of these clinics. Now I was worried; first, it was going to be a painful experience, and now the clinic we were going to was unknown? What was this going to be like for us? My thoughts were racing as I imagined what the clinic might look like in a third-world country like Pakistan without the same clinical standards we have in America.

The day came to be tested. We drove over forty minutes to the clinic. When we arrived, we walked up several flights of dark, dirty stairs to the clinic's entrance. My thoughts were whirling, but I kept trusting the Lord. We walked into a small lobby, registered, and then the nurse said, "Okay, you can go back to see the doctor." We walked around the corner, and a young, well-dressed doctor was standing there, a recent graduate from medical school. When the doctor saw me, he got noticeably excited and exclaimed, "Wow! I would be honored to test such a great evangelist!" I was shocked! He recognized me from our weekly television show, *Salvation Today*, that airs in almost every home in Pakistan. It turned out that he was also a Christian. Under my breath, I whispered, "Praise God!"

"Pastor," the doctor said, "when I test you and your wife, I will be very careful. Instead of pushing the stick far in, I will just put it in the lower part of your nose. Don't worry." He held up the test stick, and, to my amazement, it had a nice piece of cotton at the tip. Seeing that, I shouted, "Praise the Lord!" right there in that clinic. God is so good! No matter what the circumstances may be, and no matter how large or small the problem, when fear tries to grip your heart and mind, reject that fear and stand on the Word of God. God's Word says that He will never leave you nor forsake you. (See Hebrews 13:5.) Stand in faith and expect miracles to happen in the face of fear because God's Word will come to pass!

The day after getting tested for Covid, we drove to the crusade field and pulled up to see a massive crowd gathered there. More than 165,000 people were in attendance that night; to my knowledge, it was the first mass gathering of more than a hundred thousand people anywhere in the world since the pandemic had started. I reached for the microphone and began preaching the gospel. When I gave the call for salvation, more than 135,000 people stood up, surrendered their lives to Jesus Christ, and received His salvation. It was incredible!

If I had listened to fear—the relentless news reports, other people's opinions, my own imagination—we never would have done that crusade, and tens of thousands of people wouldn't have been saved that day.

Fear imprisons the soul, but faith in God's Word sets you free. To know God's holy will, you must know His holy Word. When you know what the Bible says about your situation, you know God's will, and there is no need to fear. Don't allow fear to control you. Stand on God's Word and put your trust in Him, not your circumstances, and you will see the victory, in Jesus's name!

> FEAR IMPRISONS THE SOUL, BUT FAITH IN GOD'S WORD SETS YOU FREE.

KEEP YOUR EYES ON JESUS

Let's now talk about *four keys to overcoming fear and choosing faith* instead. These keys are: (1) keep your eyes on Jesus, (2) cultivate an overcoming faith, (3) remember that God has not given us a spirit of fear, and (4) confess with your mouth.

The first key to overcoming fear is to keep your eyes on Jesus. Let's take another look at the account of Peter walking on water. *But when* [Peter] *saw that the wind was boisterous, he was afraid; and beginning to sink he cried out, saying, "Lord, save me!" And immediately Jesus stretched out His hand and caught him, and said to him, "O you of little faith, why did you doubt?"* (Matthew 14:30–31)

Earlier, we admired Peter's faith in action when Jesus told him, *"Come."* But now we see Peter's faith slip into doubt. When Peter took his eyes off Jesus and put them on his problem—the churning waves—he began to doubt. Here he was in the middle of a storm, literally walking on water, and, other than Jesus, Peter was doing something nobody else had ever done, which was miraculous! Yet, amid it all, Peter took his eyes off Jesus and started looking at the waves and the surrounding situation. The Bible says that when Peter saw the waves, he became afraid and started to sink.

Fear caused Peter to sink and spurred Jesus to say, *"O you of little faith, why did you doubt?"* Fear gripped Peter's heart and led him to doubt the word Jesus had given him. James 1:6 exhorts us, *"But let him ask in faith, with no doubting, for he who doubts is like a wave of the sea driven and tossed by the wind."*

Doubt is the issue, not a lack of faith. Many Christians think they don't have enough faith when they already have been given faith. The problem is not a lack of faith but an abundance of doubt. Peter's problem was not that he had little faith. He had enough faith to step out of the boat and start walking on the water. His problem was that he began to believe his fears more than God's Word, which is doubt. When we allow our fears and doubts to control our minds, we no longer stand on God's Word but rather on those fears, which will cause us to sink every time. Fear and doubt are not a firm foundation, but God's Word is. Fear causes doubt, but faith builds confidence; confidence in God's Word is "God-fidence."

Smith Wigglesworth once said, "There is nothing impossible with God. All the impossibility is with us when we measure God by the limitations of our unbelief."[20] When any of us takes our eyes off Jesus, it shifts our focus to our problems and the issues of life around us. Then, unbelief and doubt settle into our hearts, and we start to sink. In those moments, we must choose—will we believe God's Word or the enemy's lies? Jesus is God, and He is Lord over the wind and the waves. He is Lord over the circumstances that life throws our way. With one word, Jesus—who is the Word—can silence every storm in your life. With one word, He can calm your greatest fears and resolve a bad situation for your good. Simply keep your eyes on Him.

I used to own a sports bike and loved going fast, especially around corners. I learned right away that whatever my eyes were fixed on a corner, that was where I would end up going. It came in handy when I wanted to make sharp turns. I wouldn't look at the road directly in front of me; I would look far ahead through the curve and eventually to my exit. I couldn't make the corner if I kept my eyes on the road up close. But, if I looked ahead, I could make even the sharpest corner at extremely high speeds with no problem.

It's the same in the kingdom of God, and it's the same with faith. What you look at is where you will go. We must fix our eyes on the right target. You can either fix your eyes on your fear or stand in a position of faith, fixing your eyes on Jesus. If you fix your eyes on doubt, you enter a world of fear. But fixing your eyes on Jesus gives you courage and strength to get around life's "corners." Even the most difficult corners of life can be overcome by looking at the right target. When we keep our eyes fixed on Jesus, then, when He speaks, when He calls us, when He gives us a promise, we can stand on that promise! Why? Because Jesus is Lord! He knows the beginning from the end, and He is faithful.

---

20. GoodReads.com, "Smith Wigglesworth Quotes," https://www.goodreads.com/author/quotes/191049.Smith_Wigglesworth.

CULTIVATE OVERCOMING FAITH

The second key to overcoming fear is to cultivate overcoming faith. Fear is the enemy of faith, the antithesis of faith. Fear can cause you to destroy your dreams, desires, and God's plan for your life, but faith in God and His Word will enable you to overcome your greatest fears and obstacles. Overcoming faith defeats powerful opposition by trusting in the unseen God.

Moses started his journey in fear because he had killed an Egyptians who had beaten a Hebrew slave. In Exodus 2:15, Moses fled from the face of Pharaoh to escape punishment for this murder. However, Hebrews 11:27 tells us, *"By faith he [Moses] forsook Egypt, not fearing the wrath of the king; for he endured as seeing Him who is invisible."* This might sound like a contradiction, but it is two incidences separated by many years. In the first case, Moses fled Egypt *out of fear* for his life; forty years later, Moses forsook Egypt, *not out of fear* of Pharaoh but because he was walking in faith in an unseen God. By then, Moses knew who God was, and he knew that his destiny was to be the deliverer of God's covenant people.

OVERCOMING FAITH DEFEATS POWERFUL OPPOSITION BY TRUSTING IN THE UNSEEN GOD.

Faith often puts us into opposition against powerful forces, as Moses later faced the great army of Egypt, but his overcoming faith won the battle. Faith empowers us to obey God without fear. God's way of deliverance must be applied by faith to be effective. God delights in turning overwhelming problems into displays of His mighty power through overcoming faith.

GOD HAS NOT GIVEN US A SPIRIT OF FEAR

The third key to overcoming fear is to remember that God has not given us a spirit of fear. In 2 Timothy 1:7, Paul gives practical advice to his young protégé Timothy, reminding him, *"For God has not given us a spirit of fear, but of power and of love and of a sound mind."* Context is everything to understand a verse. In the apostle's final New Testament letter, he reflects on his real challenges—abandoned by his friends, assaulted by his foes, and alone in a Roman prison. In that solitary moment, Paul thinks about Timothy, his *"true son in the faith"* (1 Timothy 1:2). Even though Timothy is not the one in prison, he needs more than a pep talk; he needs the power of God! Paul exhorts Timothy to reject the spirit of fear from the enemy and to surrender instead to the Spirit of God who gives him power, love, and a sound mind to overcome all fear.

In the phrase *"the spirit of fear,"* the Greek word for *"fear"* is *deilia,* meaning timidity, fearfulness, and cowardice.[21] A person with a spirit of fear or timidity may be ensnared or prevented from proclaiming the gospel or upholding the truth of God's Word. It happens because of an overwhelming sense of threat or danger, causing a loss of courage. Paul was encouraging Timothy not to let a spirit of fear or shame from the enemy undermine his gifts from the Holy Spirit. *"I remind you to stir up the gift of God which is in you…. Do not be ashamed of the testimony of our Lord, nor of me His prisoner, but share with me in the sufferings for the gospel according to the power of God…"* (2 Timothy 1:6, 8). Timothy needed Paul's encouragement to stir up his gift and to go from his deepest fears to his highest faith.

God has given every Christian the spirit of power, love, and a sound mind to overcome our fears. Power is the unwavering accompaniment of the gift of the Holy Spirit. This power "casts out fear" and stimulates us to pray and cast it out of others. (See 1 John 4:18.)

---

21. *Strongs* #1167, *deilia,* https://biblehub.com/greek/1167.htm.

The Spirit also works in us with "love" and "a sound mind." God's Word assures us, *"There is no fear in love; but perfect love casts out fear, because fear involves torment. But he who fears has not been made perfect in love"* (1 John 4:18). It is God's perfect love for us that drives away our fear. Fear brings torment, but God doesn't want you to be tormented! He wants you to have power, love, and peace of mind!

> *GOD HAS GIVEN EVERY CHRISTIAN THE SPIRIT OF POWER, LOVE, AND A SOUND MIND TO OVERCOME OUR FEARS.*

What do you fear the most? Maybe you fear people or what people think about you; maybe you fear broken relationships or financial ruin. Many people are fearful of death, but Jesus has provided the answer for their freedom: *"That through death [Jesus] might destroy him who had the power of death, that is, the devil, and release those who through fear of death were all their lifetime subject to bondage"* (Hebrews 2:14–15). Whatever your fear is, Jesus Christ has already provided the answer.

OVERCOMING FINANCIAL FEARS

When we started our ministry in 2015, we were believing God for large amounts of money for our crusades. We had a few prayer partners when we began, but we had no financial partners. We pressed forward, continuing to believe in God through prayer and by doing our part. We did everything we could think of; we sent out emails and newsletters, asking people to support us financially, but it was very difficult, and financial fear haunted us.

During that first year, I struggled, constantly feeling stressed out and wondering how we would survive financially. How would we see millions of people come to Christ and fulfill the prophecies over our lives? I began to pray like this: "God, I know that You've called me, and I know that You've spoken prophetic words over me. You said we'd see millions of people saved through our ministry, but it seems so far away. It seems unattainable because I can barely raise enough money to put food on the table."

For a year, I woke up between three and five o'clock every morning, stressed out, wondering how to pay for this crusade, the next crusade, and the one after that. How would we cover our payroll and still pay rent for next month? After a year of living like that, the Holy Spirit convicted me to take a closer look at our finances; what I saw opened my eyes of faith. I prayed, "God, You provided for us every single time. Every time we needed payroll, You provided it. Every time we had a goal to raise money for a crusade, You provided. Every time we stepped out in faith, believing that You have called us to do this for your kingdom, You provided. Lord, I no longer need to be stressed out or bound in financial fear. Why? Because You are faithful to provide."

God is faithful to provide for you if you believe everything is possible. Maybe you are working hard at your job but struggling to provide for your family. Have faith in God that He will provide in unusual or unseen ways. Perhaps you are a single mother who must work to provide for your children, but if you have faith and trust in God, He will provide. Philippians 4:19 assures us, *"And my God shall supply all your need according to His riches in glory by Christ Jesus."*

CONFESS WITH YOUR MOUTH

The fourth key to overcoming fear is to confess with your mouth.

"The word is near you, in your mouth and in your heart" (that is, the word of faith which we preach): *that if you confess with your mouth the Lord Jesus and believe in your heart that God has raised Him from the dead, you will be saved.* (Romans 10:8–9)

Confession is not only what people think of at first—admission of wrongdoing. Confession is whatever you speak out loud. "Confess with your mouth" means to profess something out loud—to speak it, declare it, and to do it openly and publicly. Since God has called me to be an evangelist, when I think of confessing with our mouths, salvation always comes to mind. Remember, according to Romans 10:8–9, two things are required for salvation: *confession* and *faith*. If you *confess with your lips* that Jesus is Lord and truly *believe with your heart* that God raised Jesus from the dead, you will be saved. The outward confession must be true to what you feel in your inward heart.

It's also a confession of faith when we believe God's Word and confess it to overcome our fears. Words are containers of power that create action. *"Fight the good fight of faith, lay hold on eternal life, to which you were also called and have confessed the good confession in the presence of many witnesses"* (1 Timothy 6:12). I had to fight in faith against those financial fears early in our ministry. I confessed that God was my Provider (see Genesis 22:14), and that truth overcame the fear in my heart.

WORDS ARE CONTAINERS OF POWER THAT CREATE ACTION.

The Bible says, *"Death and life are in the power of the tongue"* (Proverbs 18:21). What you say flows from what is in your heart, for *"out of the abundance of the heart [the] mouth speaks"* (Luke 6:45). This is true in everyday life. If you speak life over your children, you'll see them prosper and have faith. You should speak encouraging words to them, such as, "You are amazing and awesome. God has a wonderful plan for you. I love you so much, and I see your talents. You can do all things in Christ." When you speak words of life this way, you will see them grow and flourish.

But speaking death over your children, including negative, angry, and evil words, can fill them with fear and even ruin their lives. The language of death says things like, "You are an idiot." "You're just not good enough to succeed." "You are a loser." With these words of rejection, don't be surprised when you see their life's value diminish as they become weak and fearful.

When you speak the Word of God over your children—and over yourself and others—you tap into the limitless power of the Holy Spirit. The Word spoken in faith in the name of Jesus overcomes insurmountable obstacles. God's Word in your mouth is as powerful as when it comes out of His mouth. Why? Because God's Word lasts forever. It is eternal. Jesus is the Word of God, who became flesh and dwelled among us. His Word is in you, and when you speak His Word, you're not just speaking a human language but the language of the Creator of the universe. It is the Word of God, and it is powerful and sharper than any two-edged sword. *"For the word of God is living and powerful, and sharper than any two-edged sword, piercing even to the division of soul and spirit, and of joints and marrow, and is a discerner of the thoughts and intents of the heart"* (Hebrews 4:12).

SAY NO TO FEAR AND YES TO FAITH

Years ago, we talked with a doctor who gives medical shots required for travel. The doctor asked me if I was on anti-anxiety medication. When I said, "No, I'm not," she told me that more than half of her patients were on anti-anxiety medicine. Many people struggle with fear, but you don't have to overcome fear with medicine. Jesus has the power to deliver you from all your fears!

Faith overcomes fear, anxiety, worry, depression, and suicidal thoughts. But how do you have faith that conquers your greatest fear? You conquer your greatest obstacles by the Word, which never fails you. The Word of God is a lamp to your feet and a light to your path. (See Psalm 119:105.) Never forget, when life seems dark and difficult, to turn to God's Word and spend time in it; it is your road map for life and will bring you many victories. The Word of God trumps all fear. You must say no to fear and doubt if you want great faith!

I love this story of faith over fear. "John Wesley, the founder of the Methodist Church, set out for America in 1735, enthused at the idea of preaching the gospel to Native Americans. During the transatlantic voyage, his ship was caught in a terrifying storm. John was afraid, but as the storm raged, he witnessed a worship service held by a group of German Moravians when a huge wave engulfed the ship and water poured down into the cabins. While the English passengers screamed in terror, the Moravians continued their singing, seemingly untroubled by the present mortal danger. Afterward, when Wesley asked one of the Moravians if they had been afraid, the Germans replied that not even the women and children had been afraid. None of them was afraid to die."[22] Jesus had replaced their fear with His Spirit and His love.

The storms of life will never trump Jesus's power because the storms of life bow to Him. Yes, you will face storms in life, but you will find that Jesus is there with you *in* the storms, and that He is Lord *over* the storms. If you keep your eyes fixed on Jesus, you will have the proper perspective and see the victory. He is Lord, and His Word is truth. It never returns void! "*So shall My word be that goes forth from My mouth; it*

---

22. Glenn M. Wagner, "Courage to Face Our Fears," October 7, 2020, Michigan Conference: The United Methodist Church, https://michiganumc.org/courage-to-face-our-fears/#:~:text=Wesley%20remembered%20the%20role%20of,in%20coping%20with%20 our%20fears.

shall not return to Me void, but it shall accomplish what I please, and it shall prosper in the thing for which I sent it" (Isaiah 55:11).

THE STORMS OF LIFE WILL NEVER TRUMP JESUS'S POWER BECAUSE THE STORMS OF LIFE BOW TO HIM.

SEVEN

OVERCOME EVERY ATTACK OF THE ENEMY

"I'm not afraid of the devil...the devil is afraid of me!"[23]

—*Reinhard Bonnke*

*"I also say to you that you are Peter, and on this rock
I will build My church, and the gates of Hades [hell]
shall not prevail against it."*

—Matthew 16:18

Jesus and His disciples came into the Caesarea Philippi region of Israel, a mostly pagan city of Greeks, Romans, and Jews, sitting at the crossroads about forty miles north of the Sea of Galilee. In Matthew,

---

23. Reinhard Bonnke, "I'm not afraid of the Devil, he's afraid of me," Air Media House, posted June 15, 2023, YouTube shorts, https://youtube.com/shorts/UNypt7OjBt4?si=yGOwOrJOYMq3VdG_.

chapter 16, we see that the stage is set for one of the greatest conversations recorded between Jesus and His disciples that would reveal who Jesus is and what He came to do. As He often did, Jesus started the conversation with a question for His disciples, asking, *"Who do men say that I, the Son of Man, am?"* (Matthew 16:13). With some uncertainty, several disciples responded, "John the Baptist," "Elijah," "Jeremiah," or "One of the other prophets." (See verse 14.) Putting pressure on them, Jesus asked a more penetrating question: *"Who do **you** say that I am?"* (verse 15).

I don't think it's a coincidence that Jesus and His disciples were standing in the vicinity of the pagan temple in Caesarea Philippi built to honor the Roman emperor Caesar Augustus, the adopted son of Julius Caesar. The Romans considered both Caesars to be gods, yet now these mere men were dead. When Peter answered Jesus's question, *"Who do **you** say that I am?"* near that temple, he spoke an eternal truth revealed to him by the Father. Peter declared, *"You are **the Christ**, the **Son of the living God**"* (Matthew 16:16).

Peter made the starkest contrast possible: two men who falsely believed they were deities but were now dead and gone, compared to Jesus the Messiah, *the Christ*, the Son of *the eternal, living God*. Jesus commended Peter for his divine revelation, saying to him, *"Blessed are you, Simon Bar-Jonah, for flesh and blood has not revealed this to you, but My Father who is in heaven. And I also say to you that you are Peter, and on this rock, I will build My church, and the gates of Hades shall not prevail against it"* (Matthew 16:17–18).

BUILD ON THE ROCK

Years ago, the Lord revealed to me that I didn't clearly understand the true meaning of Matthew 16:18: *"You are Peter, and on this rock, I will build My church, and the gates of Hades shall not prevail against it."* After I had studied this verse more closely, God showed me three important points in this verse for overcoming Satan and the gates of hell.

1. JESUS IS OUR ONLY FOUNDATION

The verse begins, *"You are Peter* [petros], *and on this rock* [petra], *I will build my church."* There has been debate over the centuries concerning the exact meaning of these words. Jesus commended Peter and called him *petros,* which in Greek is *little stone,* Jesus's name for Peter since the day he became a disciple. Then, the Lord went on to say, *"...and on this petra* (which means giant stone) *I will build my church."*

In 1 Corinthians 3:11, Paul points to Jesus Christ as the foundation of our faith, saying, *"For no other foundation can anyone lay than that which is laid, which is Jesus Christ."* Then, in 1 Corinthians 10:4, Paul writes of Christ as the Rock: *"They drank of that spiritual Rock that followed them, and that Rock was Christ."* Jesus Christ is the only foundation or cornerstone of the church. Peter was a strong leader among the apostles, but Jesus was saying, in effect, "You are Peter, but it is the *revelation* that I am the Christ that is the *rock* on which I will build My church, and the gates of hell will not prevail against it!"

JESUS CHRIST IS THE ONLY FOUNDATION OR CORNERSTONE OF THE CHURCH.

2. THIS VERSE IDENTIFIES BELIEVERS AS THE CHURCH

Of course, Jesus is not talking about physical church buildings, as I once assumed. *You and I* are the church, the body of Christ, the collective worldwide church. If you are a born-again believer in Jesus Christ as the Son of God and the Savior of the world, then we are part of the same universal church. However, in earlier years, I thought that the church Jesus was referring to in this verse were church buildings that had physical gates on them. You know, in Pakistan, where I preach most of the time, most churches must build a wall around the church property for protection from potential invaders and attackers. In one section of the wall, they have a giant metal gate that can open for cars to enter the church property, but every Sunday, those gates are locked, and the only opening is one large enough for churchgoers to walk through.

They usually have a small door built into the gates where armed guards carrying AK-47 machine guns keep watch. Most of the time, the armed guards use metal detectors to prevent attacks against the churches because suicide bombers and radical gunmen are not uncommon in Pakistan. That is why I had a picture in my mind of the gates on the church with Satan constantly pounding against them. Then I realized that it was *the exact opposite* of what occurs. It's not physical church gates; it's spiritual gates; it's hell's gates. And those gates will never prevail against or overcome the church of Jesus Christ.

3. THE GATES OF HELL WILL NOT PREVAIL AGAINST THE CHURCH

"I will build My church, and the gates of Hades shall not prevail against it" (Matthew 16:18). This verse captures what we call spiritual warfare. Jesus explains that there are two spiritual kingdoms—the kingdom of heaven and the kingdom of darkness—at war with one another.

Unfortunately, too many people—believers and unbelievers alike—have a false theology about the kingdom of heaven and the kingdom of darkness. In their unbiblical perspective, they believe that God and the devil are *equal* opposites at war. This is false; the devil could never be an equal to God.

First of all, God is all-powerful, and the devil cannot even stand in His presence without God's permission. In addition, Satan is a being who was *created* by God as the archangel Lucifer; he rebelled against God's authority and was kicked out of heaven. As punishment for his disobedience and the grave dishonoring of his angelic post, God cast Lucifer out of heaven by hurling him and his army of fallen angels to earth (see Isaiah 14:15; Revelation 12:9) and condemning them ultimately to hell. (See Matthew 25:41.) The kingdom of heaven is more powerful than the kingdom of darkness, for heaven is eternal, but the kingdom of darkness is temporal.

The Word of God assures us that the gates of hell will not prevail against us—you and me, the body of Jesus Christ. Therefore, it means that we are the ones who should be on the offensive! We should be taking territory against the gates of hell. We are overcomers. We are the ones taking back territory from Satan's domain! Jesus has given us the authority that God originally gave to Adam in Genesis 1:26, when He said, "*Let Us make man in Our image, according to Our likeness; let them have dominion....*" Adam lost his authority to the devil when he sinned, but we regained that authority in Jesus Christ. When Jesus rose from the dead victorious, He held the keys to death, hell, and the grave! And because Jesus rose, we rose to new life with Him. "*Just as Christ was raised from the dead by the glory of the Father, even so we should also walk in newness of life*" (Romans 6:4).

THE WORD OF GOD ASSURES US THAT THE GATES OF HELL WILL NOT PREVAIL AGAINST US—YOU AND ME, THE BODY OF JESUS CHRIST.

Since the devil is already defeated, in Jesus's name, you and I can enter into victory by the blood of Jesus and through the power of the gospel and the resurrection. Praise God! We are given a position of authority in Jesus Christ, being grafted into the family of God. (See Romans 11:17.)

Christian, listen! Don't just sit back and say, "The devil is always attacking me, and I'm feeling so defeated." No! In the name of Jesus, you are called to be victorious. You are called to be an overcomer! You are called to speak out the truth of your victory! *"For whatever is born of God overcomes the world. And this is the victory that has overcome the world— our faith. Who is he who overcomes the world, but he who believes that Jesus is the Son of God?"* (1 John 5:4–6).

Too many Christians teach spiritual warfare as though the devil is always attacking us, always beating us down, and that we are weak and powerless to resist. It's as if they are saying, "If we don't watch out, the devil might jump out and get us." I've heard Christians say things like, "I've been under such an attack from the enemy, and I don't know what to do. I'm not strong enough for his attacks." But that is not true! God's will for you is not to be overrun by the enemy but to overcome the enemy in Jesus's name. In Christ, we're not called to be on the defensive; we're called to be on the offensive! We're called to take dominion like a soldier takes land back from the enemy. We're called to overcome, in Jesus's name!

BE STRONG IN THE LORD

We are not ignorant of Satan's plans; we know that the devil still attacks the church, Christ's body. Paul warns us in Ephesians 6 that we are at war, not against flesh and blood, but against spiritual wickedness—principalities, powers, and rulers of darkness: *"For we do not wrestle against flesh and blood, but against principalities, against powers, against the rulers of the darkness of this age, against spiritual hosts of wickedness in the heavenly places"* (Ephesians 6:12).

Paul also gives us the keys to being winners and not losers in this spiritual battle against the enemy: *"Finally, my brethren, **be strong in the Lord** and in the power of His might. Put on the whole armor of God, that you may be able to stand against the wiles of the devil"* (Ephesians 6:10–11). I could preach a whole message right here! *Be strong in the Lord!* Don't be weak in the Lord. Don't allow the devil to push you around. Don't just lie down and let the devil run over you. *Be strong in the Lord and in the power of His might.* How? By obeying the Word and putting on the spiritual armor that God has given us!

Do we put on the whole armor of God so that we can continue to be beaten up and attacked by the devil? No, that's not what it says. It says to put on the whole armor of God so you *"might be able to stand against the wiles of the devil."* Sure, the devil has some tactics, but God has provided us with the power of the Holy Spirit and the spiritual armor to overcome him!

Too often, when Christians read in Ephesians 6:12 about principalities, powers, and spiritual hosts of wickedness, they become afraid and take this verse completely out of context. They think of it as describing a bad, scary movie. When you believe false interpretations of the Scriptures, it positions you in a weak place without power or spiritual strength. Some people misunderstand these words because they focus more on the enemy than on the power of

God. They live by fear, not by faith. Sadly, they believe the devil will overtake them by breaking their gates. Be assured that our gates will not come crashing down! With faith, we will attack the enemy of our soul, and the gates of hell will not prevail against us, the church!

HAVING DONE ALL, STAND

Why do we put on the armor of God? It is so that we will be able to *stand against* the enemy. "*Therefore take up the whole armor of God, that you may be able to withstand in the evil day, and having done all,* **to stand**" (Ephesians 6:13). You don't have to be beaten up by the devil! You can stand strong in the Lord and arm yourself with the power of God, standing against all the treachery of the enemy.

"**Stand therefore***, having girded your waist with truth, having put on the breastplate of righteousness, and having shod your feet with the preparation of the gospel of peace*" (verses 14–15). This is the third time Paul calls believers to *stand firm* as though facing a military general. God commands His troops of saints to stand firm, immovable and steadfast, by living the obedient life of the Commander of hosts, the King of glory, and by embracing the life empowered by the Holy Spirit to conquer every enemy in the name of Jesus. So, Christian, stand firm!

God calls us to take an offensive stand against the enemy, yet He has provided us with both offensive and defensive armor, giving us weapons we will need for any kind of battle. Going into the promised land is an illustration of offensive warfare. When the Israelites entered the promised land, they were certainly on the offensive side of war. God went before them into battle as they conquered the land, one city at a time. Second Corinthians gives us direction for offensive warfare: "*For the weapons of our warfare are not carnal but mighty in God for pulling down strongholds, casting down arguments and every high thing that exalts itself against the knowledge of God, bringing every thought into captivity to the obedience of Christ"* (2 Corinthians 10:4–5). We are to be **mighty** in God *to **pull down*** strongholds, ***cast down*** arguments, and bring all of our thoughts ***into captivity***. Those are offensive weapons from a mighty God!

GOD COMMANDS HIS TROOPS OF SAINTS TO STAND FIRM, IMMOVABLE AND STEADFAST.

PUT ON THE WHOLE ARMOR OF GOD

In Ephesians 6:14–17, Paul begins to list the different aspects of the supernatural armor of God:

> *Stand therefore, having girded your waist with truth, having put on the breastplate of righteousness, and having shod your feet with the preparation of the gospel of peace; above all, taking the shield of faith with which you will be able to quench all the fiery darts of the wicked one. And take the helmet of salvation, and the sword of the Spirit, which is the word of God.*

Gird your waist with truth—the belt of truth is first on the list of the armor of God. You may be wondering why Paul started with the belt. Just as a belt is worn close to the body, we should hold God's truth close to our hearts and allow it to surround us. The belt of truth protects us and prepares us for the spiritual battle that is part of every Christian's life. Jesus defined Himself as *"the way, the truth, and the life"* (John 14:6). He also defined God's Word as truth: *"Sanctify them by Your truth. Your word is truth"* (John 17:17). In a world that drifts without absolutes,

God's truth is our anchor! When we remain in His Word, we can distinguish what is true from the enemy's lies.

Put on the breastplate of righteousness—the warrior's breastplate is the protector of the heart and other vital organs. The breastplate of righteousness is given to us because of our right standing with God through salvation in Jesus Christ. "*For He made Him* [Jesus] *who knew no sin to be sin for us, that **we might become the righteousness of God** in Him*" (2 Corinthians 5:21). This is not our own earned righteousness, or a feeling of righteousness, but righteousness received by faith in Jesus Christ alone. It gives us a deep sense of confidence in our position in God through His Son Jesus. Martyn Lloyd-Jones, a well-known early pastor at Westminster Chapel in London, wrote, "Thank God for experiences, but do not rely on them. You do not put on the 'breastplate of experiences'; you put on the breastplate of 'righteousness.'"

Pursuing the righteousness of God also means putting Him at the center of our lives. God takes pleasure in those who pursue righteousness. "*The LORD detests the way of the wicked, but he loves those who pursue righteousness*" (Proverbs 15:9 NIV). He delights when we walk rightly before Him as we rely on the power of the Holy Spirit. "*I will put My Spirit within you and cause you to walk in My statutes, and you will keep My judgments and do them*" (Ezekiel 36:27).

Having shod your feet with the preparation of the gospel of peace—the Greek word for "*shod*" is *hupodeo* from the words *hupó*, meaning "under," and *déo*, meaning "to bind."[24] The two words together mean "to bind under," such as, to bind under one's feet, as putting on shoes or sandals. To stand firm, a soldier must have secure footing. For the Roman soldier, the nails or cleats on the soles of his shoes provided firm footing in rough terrain. For the

---

24. *Strong's* #5265, *hupodeo*, https://www.bibletools.org/index.cfm/fuseaction/Lexicon.show/ID/G5265/hupodeo.htm.

Christian soldier, our firm footing is the good news that speaks peace just as the Lord Jesus made peace between us and the Father by the blood of His cross.

The gospel of peace communicates the good news that, through Christ, believers are at peace with God, and He is on their side. (See Romans 5:6–10.) This confidence in divine support allows the believer to stand firm. *"And the peace of God, which surpasses all understanding, will guard your hearts and minds through Christ Jesus"* (Philippians 4:7). It requires humility and courage to experience God's peace, seeking beyond the mere abilities of our own understanding. Finding peace of mind can be one of the greatest weapons in our battles.

ABOVE ALL, TAKE UP THE SHIELD OF FAITH

Taking the shield of faith—*"Above all, taking the shield of faith with which you will be able to quench* [extinguish] *all the fiery darts of the wicked one"* (Ephesians 6:16). Stop for a minute and say this with me: "Above all! Above everything else! Above everything, *have faith!*" We must never forget the importance and power of supernatural faith. The verse says "take up" that shield. Make the decision to take it up into your battle. With the shield of faith, you will be able to quench or extinguish *all* of the flaming darts the enemy shoots at you! How many? *All* of them will be quenched in Jesus's name!

In Roman times there were two kinds of shields that soldiers used. The first one was called the *parma* shield. It was a smaller, lightweight shield that the soldier could move around to protect specific parts of his body. It could also be used offensively to drive back the enemy in hand-to-hand combat. "The parma was about three feet in diameter and the lighter of the two shields. But it was not the shield of choice for the Roman legion. Their favorite shield was the *scutum*, which was made by gluing several layers of wood together the way plywood is made today. It was then covered with leather for extra protection and durability. Due to its size and weight, the soldier couldn't move this shield around very well, so, once he was in position, he would plant it on the ground and crouch behind it for protection."[25] The Christian's shield of faith will effectively counteract all of Satan's fiery missiles not only by deflecting them but also by quenching the flames to prevent them from spreading.

> *WITH THE SHIELD OF FAITH, YOU WILL BE ABLE TO QUENCH OR EXTINGUISH ALL OF THE FLAMING DARTS THE ENEMY SHOOTS AT YOU!*

You must understand that the enemy will try to stop your growth in Christ by convincing you to doubt God's Word and lose faith. That is why the Bible teaches that faith is your shield, countering every satanic projectile fired against you. You don't have to live in defeat. You don't have to live under constant attack by the enemy. God has given you a plan to be victorious in Jesus's name. Hallelujah!

Taking up the shield of faith is the key to winning every battle! Faith that obeys makes you like an impregnable castle wall. *"And this is the victory that has overcome the world—our faith"* (1 John 5:4). Faith is the expression of a defensive and offensive force against the world's forces. Faith in God will make you victorious over every attack of the enemy, so don't lay down your shield. Don't lay down your faith and allow the enemy to defeat you. Instead, stand up in faith, knowing that God is for you, and if He is for you, who can be against you? (See Romans 8:31.)

---

25. Jeremy Myers, "Taking Up the Shield of Faith (Ephesians 6:16)," Redeeming God, https://redeeminggod.com/ephesians_6_16/.

THE HELMET AND THE SWORD

Take up the helmet of salvation—when a soldier suited up for battle, the helmet was the last piece of armor to go on. A helmet is vital for survival in war, protecting the brain, which is the command center of the body. The rest of the armor would be of little use if the head was critically injured. Though Goliath was wearing his helmet, with a slingshot and a rock, David killed him. Not all helmets can protect you; you need the helmet of salvation.

When you trust the Lord, stand on His Word, and have faith, you will move mountains in the name above all other names, Jesus. It doesn't work for you if you don't have the helmet of salvation. Salvation is vital. However, in this verse, Paul is not just talking about our initial salvation; he is also talking about God as his *complete* salvation, restoration, and deliverance.

The Old Testament gives us many examples of God's salvation in rescuing those He loved. Moses told the Israelites not to fear the Egyptians in the coming battle. *"And Moses said to the people, 'Do not be afraid. Stand still, and see **the salvation** of the LORD, which He will accomplish for you today'"* (Exodus 14:13).

David fought many battles as a servant to Saul and as the King of Israel. Through those battles, he learned that God was his salvation. *"The LORD is my light and my salvation; whom shall I fear? The LORD is the strength of my life; of whom shall I be afraid?"* (Psalm 27:1). *"Truly he is my rock and my salvation; he is my fortress; I will never be shaken"* (Psalm 62:2 NIV). *"He only is my rock and my salvation; He is my defense; I shall not be greatly moved"* (Psalm 62:2). *"In God is my salvation and my glory; the rock of my strength, and my refuge, is in God"* (Psalm 62:7). God is your salvation, a rock and a fortress that strengthens you in spiritual conflicts. With faith in God, you will never be shaken and never be moved, unlike those who are easily shaken because they are faithless. With God's salvation, we can expect restoration, favor, and security.

[Take up] *the sword of the Spirit, which is the Word [rhema] of* **God**—this is the final act of readiness in preparation for combat. The sword of the Spirit is different. It doesn't protect; it maims. It isn't passive; it's active. It is intended for combat—a weapon for frontline spiritual warfare. Paul uses the Greek word *rhema* in this verse to indicate the sword represents God's spoken Word. The spoken Word of God has the power to confront and overpower the enemy.

When the Holy Spirit led Jesus into the desert, the enemy came to do battle, and Jesus came with a sword, the Word. Jesus used *rhema* to refute Satan's temptation to turn the stones into bread. *"If you are the Son of God, command that these stones become bread"* (Matthew 4:3), Satan taunted him. Jesus charged forward with the Word of God and answered him, *"Man shall not live by bread alone, but by every word [rhema] that proceeds from the mouth of God"* (Matthew 4:4). People need more than bread for their life; they must feed on every Word of God. (See Matthew 4:1–11.) Watching the life of Jesus, observing His conflict with Satan and the scribes and Pharisees, teaches us how to wield the sword of God's Word with power and conviction. The Word of God is a sword that pierces hearts and confounds the enemy!

POWERFUL WARRIORS IN GOD'S KINGDOM ARE FAMILIAR WITH THE WORD AND WILL SPEAK IT WITH FAITH AND CONVICTION.

Church, God is looking for a people who will defeat their spiritual opponents and tear off the devil's equipment and armor so that he will be disgraced. Powerful warriors in God's kingdom are familiar with the Word and will speak it with faith and conviction. When you take up the shield of faith and brandish the sword of God's Word, you possess mighty weapons of warfare that cannot be defeated!

My friends, the next time you encounter a spiritual battle—with health, relationships, finances, or lies from the devil—stand in faith that God is with you, put on the whole armor of God provided for you, and speak His Word out loud over your situation. You will defeat every onslaught of the enemy in Jesus's name!

EIGHT

THE POWER
TO BE VICTORIOUS

"The devil knows if he can capture your thought life, he has
won a mighty victory over you."[26]
—*Smith Wigglesworth*

"*Submit to God. Resist the devil and he will flee from you.*"
—James 4:7

The world system aligned against God and His people is deceived
into thinking it has a defense against God's omnipotent weapons.
However, the defeat of every "Goliath" (that fails to bow the knee and
receive Christ as Savior) is sure! The Word of God, the power of the
Holy Spirit, and faith will defeat every Goliath. It may not look that

---

26. Smith Wigglesworth, *Greater Works* (New Kensington, PA: Whitaker House, 2000),
25.

way in your life today, but you know the end of the story! The God who ensured the victory for David will do the same for you when you speak the Word of God in faith.

The victory of David over Goliath is one of the most memorable scenes in the Bible. Many of us learned the story as children: the mighty giant clothed in armor being defeated by a shepherd boy with his little slingshot and five stones. But the real meaning of the David and Goliath story is that David was a young man of great faith who had no fear. Though just a boy at the time, he had supernatural faith in the power and honor of his God.

The Philistines were at war with Israel. Goliath stepped forward on the battlefield so all the Israelites could see him and called out to Israel's ranks, *"Why have you come out to line up for battle? Am I not a Philistine, and you the servants of Saul? Choose a man for yourselves, and let him come down to me. If he is able to fight with me and kill me, then we will be your servants. But if I prevail against him and kill him, then you shall be our servants and serve us"* (1 Samuel 17:8–9). Goliath was saying, "I defy you, Israel. Get me a man, and let's fight it out." David responded, asking one of the soldiers nearby, *"Who is this uncircumcised Philistine, that he should defy the armies of the living God?"* (verse 26). Minutes later, David told King Saul, *"Let no man's heart fail because of him; your servant will go and fight with this Philistine"* (verse 32). Saul was incredulous, saying, *"You are not able to go against this Philistine to fight with him; for you are a youth, and he a man of war from his youth"* (verse 33). Saul didn't think David had a chance, and he didn't think Israel had a chance, but David had a history with God and His delivering power—he knew God was with him.

I love David's response:

> *"Your servant has killed both lion and bear; and this uncircumcised Philistine will be like one of them, seeing he has defied the armies of*

the living God...The LORD, *who delivered me from the paw of the lion and from the paw of the bear, He will deliver me from the hand of this Philistine."* (verses 36, 37)

David's faith wasn't in his size or his age; neither was his faith in Saul's armor or sword. David's real strength and power were in *the living God* and the power of the Word. Remember, when you believe something, it manifests out of your mouth. Faith is always linked to the tongue. David said, in effect, "I've got one word for you, Goliath!"

You come to me with a sword, with a spear, and with a javelin. But I come to you in the name of the LORD *of hosts, the God of the armies of Israel, whom you have defied. This day the* LORD *will deliver you into my hand, and I will strike you and take your head from you. And this day I will give the carcasses of the camp of the Philistines to the birds of the air and the wild beasts of the earth, that all the earth may know that there is a God in Israel.* (1 Samuel 17:45–46)

On that day, David confessed that there was a God in heaven.

What a perfect lesson for us! We have the authority to say to the enemy that comes against us, "God is going to conquer you today. Jesus's name is the name above all names. I come to you in that name, the name of the Lord of hosts, the God of Israel. The name that will cause every knee to bow and every tongue to confess that Jesus Christ is Lord." We can stand before our enemy, Satan, and win our battles with faith in the power of God!

OVERCOMING THE ENEMY'S DECEPTION

Since the garden of Eden, Satan's most insidious strategy against God's people has been deception. *"Now the serpent was more cunning than any beast of the field which the* LORD *God had made"* (Genesis

3:1). Though neither the devil nor Satan is mentioned in the garden account, Revelation 12:9 confirms who the serpent was: *"The great dragon was cast out, that serpent of old, called the Devil and Satan, who deceives the whole world."* According to Genesis 3, Satan's plan against Adam and Eve was to twist God's words so that Eve would embrace a lie instead of God's truth. The devil was manipulative, treacherous, and crafty. *"And he said to the woman, 'Has God indeed said, "You shall not eat of every tree of the garden"?...You will not surely die. For God knows that in the day you eat of it your eyes will be opened, and you will be like God, knowing good and evil'"* (Genesis 3:1, 4–5). These are the first words of Satan on the earth, and they are craftily constructed to make Eve doubt the Word of God. "You will be like God"—that was always Satan's desire, and now he imposes that desire upon Adam and Eve to be like God.

SINCE THE GARDEN OF EDEN, SATAN'S MOST INSIDIOUS STRATEGY AGAINST GOD'S PEOPLE HAS BEEN DECEPTION.

In the middle of that short dialogue, Eve says, *"God has said, 'You shall not eat it, nor shall you touch it, lest you die'"* (Genesis 3:3). Eve also added to and changed God's Word. Once you have treated God's Word this way, you are wide open for the devil's final deception. Eve saw that the fruit was *"good for food,...pleasant to the eyes, and...desirable to make one wise"* (Genesis 3:6). She had to choose: God's Word or Satan's word? She rejected God's Word and believed Satan's lie. The deception worked, and sin and destruction were the result. In thousands of years, the enemy's tactics haven't changed. Satan will always twist the Word of God with his lies and deception.

In the gospel of John, Jesus tells us that Satan is a murderer and that he has *no truth* in him. He is a liar and the father of all lies. Jesus scolds the Pharisees with these words: *"He [Satan] was a murderer from the beginning, and does not stand in the truth, because there is no truth in him. When he speaks a lie, he speaks from his own resources, for he is a liar and the father of it"* (John 8:44). So, how does the enemy lie to us? He taunts us in our thoughts just like Goliath taunted the Israelite soldiers with his words. Paul calls this spiritual attack a part of our warfare.

*"For the weapons of **our warfare** are not carnal but mighty in God for pulling down strongholds, **casting down arguments** and every high thing that exalts itself against the knowledge of God, bringing **every thought into captivity** to the obedience of Christ."*

(2 Corinthians 10:4–5)

Paul knew that we would face a battle of evil lies that come against God's Word. The devil wants to torment us with thoughts of failure and defeat to try to destroy our faith in Jesus. It's the sword of the Spirit, the mighty Word of God, that gives us the power to cast down the enemy's arguments against us. Once we decide to take every thought captive and make it obedient to Christ, we will start to see victory. You must know your enemy, believe that the Word of God is the truth, hold on to the promises of God's Word, and never surrender to the enemy. Knowing God's Word and having faith in it is the key to our victory over the enemy!

OVERCOMING NEGATIVE THOUGHTS

Years ago, I experienced an attack of negative thoughts that seemed overwhelming. Shortly after graduating from Bible college, I was hired as an executive assistant to evangelist Daniel Kolenda of Christ For the Nations in Dallas. It was the answer to a prophetic word that I would work for Daniel that had been spoken over me a few years earlier. Initially, it was a very challenging job because I had never done administrative work before. I didn't think I was wired that way, but Daniel took a chance on me anyway.

The first few months were really tough. I felt like a failure every day, not because of anything Daniel said to me, but because I didn't believe I could do the job or that I was qualified for the position. At the end of each day, I was afraid that I would be fired or forced to quit because of my inadequacy. Thoughts of failure overwhelmed me: "I'm not good enough, and I'm not going to make it." "I'm going to mess up and get fired." I'm not organized enough; I can't do this." The words echoed through my mind until I was locked into a mind-set of failure, and my faith was at its lowest. I began to believe the enemy's lies, falling prey to deception, which is his strongest tool to ruin people's lives.

Listening to, dwelling on, and then speaking negative thoughts is like prophesying doom over your life, and guess what happens? *"For as he* [a man] *thinks in his heart, so is he"* (Proverbs 23:7). Watch how you think; these thoughts become your words, and your words, combined with your actions, become your destiny. What you say can become what you are. Remember, your words have power because *"death and life are in the power of the tongue"* (Proverbs 18:21). When you start speaking words of unbelief, what happens? It's as though your faith is slowly slipping away.

LISTENING TO, DWELLING ON, AND THEN
SPEAKING NEGATIVE THOUGHTS IS LIKE
PROPHESYING DOOM OVER YOUR LIFE.

CHOOSE FAITH OVER DOUBT

Driving to Daniel's office one morning, I was so overcome by thoughts of doubt and unbelief concerning my job that I decided to give my notice as soon as I arrived. Suddenly, I remembered the prophetic words spoken over my life about working for Daniel Kolenda and Reinhard Bonnke's ministry. I recalled Daniel's words of encouragement that he would train me in my calling as an evangelist. Sitting at a red light in my car, I chose faith over doubt. The memory of God's promises filled my mind, and faith rose in my spirit. I cast down those negative thoughts, proclaimed faith over my situation, and declared freedom from the enemy's lies, in Jesus's name.

I shouted, "In the name of Jesus, devil, I am finished listening to your lies! I rebuke you and your lies in the name of Jesus Christ. God has not brought me here to fail; He's called me here to succeed. God has not called me to do a bad job but to do a good job. I'm going to be a great assistant and a great asset to Daniel. I will win and not lose because I'm the head, not the tail. I'm above and not beneath." (See Deuteronomy 28:13.)

Over the next few days, I continued to speak faith over my situation and to cast down those lying thoughts from Satan. The Holy Spirit strengthened me to overcome the enemy and to develop a heavenly mindset fixed on the truth of God's Word. I realized I could trust in Jesus to overcome the challenges of my job assignments. I spoke the Word out loud daily, saying, *"I can do all things through Christ who strengthens me"* (Philippians 4:13). I was learning that guarding your mind is a biblical principle to follow, and that God had promised to give me peace. *"And the peace of God, which transcends all understanding, will guard your hearts and your minds through Christ Jesus"* (Philippians 4:7).

RENEWING YOUR MIND HAS TRANSFORMATIVE POWER IN YOUR OUTLOOK.

Something changed in my spirit and my attitude. It was as though my mind was unlocked. I began to comprehend my administrative tasks like never before. Faith empowered me, and I spoke with greater confidence. Instead of always being worried, downcast, and depressed about not making it, I could see that the Holy Spirit was with me, and I knew that *"He who is in [me] is greater than he who is in the world"* (1 John 4:4). It wasn't me, but God's grace as if a wind of the Spirit came over me. I thank God for helping me to reverse my negative direction.

The Bible says that renewing your mind has transformative power in your outlook. Paul wrote, *"And do not be conformed to this world, but be transformed by the renewing of your mind, that you may prove what is that good and acceptable and perfect will of God"* (Romans 12:2). We are wise to agree with Paul. Kenneth Hagin wrote, "God's Word is our infallible guide! We need to renew our minds with God's irresistible Word. Let's take our position with God's Word as our weapon and refuge, for His Word will never fail us!"[27] William Branham once said, "To be God, He has to stand behind everything He says in His Word. And that's exactly where my faith rests, upon God's spoken Word." If you stand by God's Word, He will cause His Word to empower your life.

DON'T BLAME EVERYTHING ON THE DEVIL

Before we go any farther with spiritual warfare, there is one thing we need to get right: we need to stop blaming everything on the devil.

---

27. Rev. Kenneth W. Hagin, "What Are You Saying?" Kenneth Hagin Ministries, https://www.rhema.org/index.php?option=com_content&view=article&id=264:what-are-you-saying&catid=51&Itemid=139.

What do I mean by that? Some Christians exalt the devil by giving him too much credit for what happens in their lives. They go through life saying things like, "I got a flat tire because of the devil." My response? "It wasn't the devil; it was driving your car over a nail that caused the flat." Don't blame it on the devil; put in some elbow grease, even in your spiritual life. It is spiritual laziness when we blame everything on the enemy. You have to take some responsibility for your own life. Maybe you wonder why you are gaining weight. Don't blame the devil; start eating healthier and exercising, and you will achieve some important personal goals. Some things are just normal things that we go through in life. We overcome those things by using wisdom and common sense.

A young woman once came up to me for prayer, saying the devil had been attacking her health. "How is the devil attacking you?" I asked. "With headaches," she answered. "Every day I wake up with horrible headaches, and I know it's from the devil." So, I asked, "How much water do you drink daily?" "Actually," she responded, "I don't drink much water at all." She started increasing her daily water intake, and, to her amazement, the headaches left.

You see, not every negative thing is the devil. Often, we just need to stop being lazy and change our bad habits, taking care of our lives and our bodies the way God intended us to do in the first place. That's not to say the enemy isn't real or that he doesn't attack. He does attack; but we must stop exalting the enemy over our situations and an instead exalt Jesus, who is much bigger than the devil.

DELIVERANCE IN SRI LANKA

"Be sober, be vigilant; because your adversary the devil walks about like a roaring lion, seeking whom he may devour" (1 Peter 5:8). Most people stop right there and think about the big, bad, roaring devil

and worry about what he might do to them. But in the very next verse, we have the answer to the roaring lion, the devil: *"Resist him, steadfast in the faith"* (verse 9). James 4:7 also gives us the answer: *"Submit to God. Resist the devil, and* **he will flee from you.***"* That's a promise from God. When you submit yourself to almighty God in faith, you have all the power you need to resist the devil...and he will flee! You will not lose the fight or succumb to temptation. If you have faith, you can survive and overcome anything the enemy throws at you.

Some unbelievers, probably without knowing it, have surrendered their hearts to Satan's influence to the point where deliverance by the Holy Spirit is needed. That is why Jesus tells us that we have the authority to "cast out devils" in Jesus's name. (See Mark 16:17–18.)

WHEN YOU SUBMIT YOURSELF TO ALMIGHTY GOD IN FAITH, YOU HAVE ALL THE POWER YOU NEED TO RESIST THE DEVIL.

In 2016, we were conducting a multi-day crusade in the mountains of Sri Lanka. These were very special meetings for us, not because of the crowd size but because of how unreached the people were. The village was situated on a tea plantation in the mountains of Sri Lanka with a total population of 3,000, and not one of them was a Christian. The village was so remote and primitive that the people had never even heard of the gospel. Every night, we preached the good news of Jesus and led hundreds of people to Christ. We would also share that Jesus Christ was their Healer and that He could deliver them from evil spirits. Then we would pray for the sick, and Jesus would do mighty miracles. At the end of each meeting, we asked the people to come forward to testify of how Jesus had healed them.

On the third night, while I preached the gospel on that mountainside, a Hindu family from the village was sitting at home in their living room listening to the loudspeaker from the crusade. We always broadcast our crusades into the surrounding area so that even those who aren't present at the meetings can hear. While I was preaching about Jesus, the family's teenage daughter fell on the floor of their house and started foaming at the mouth, slithering like a snake on the floor, and growling like a dog.

The family heard me tell everyone in the village that Jesus is the Healer and that He can set anyone free from evil spirits, so they decided to bring their daughter to the crusade. First, they tried to have her take a seat at the back of the crusade tent. But as soon as she sat down, she started kicking and then throwing chairs everywhere, causing a huge scene. At the time, Amanda, who was standing toward the back of the crowd, asked some pastors who had come with us to take the young woman outside and pray for her. They took her outside and started to pray for Jesus to set her free.

As soon as I finished my message, I began praying for the sick and then taking testimonies of healings. To my surprise, the teenage girl was the first person in line to share her story. Only one problem—the pastors couldn't deliver her from the demon; and when she got on stage in front of everyone, she fell again and started kicking and screaming. Now, I knew I needed the Lord to show up!

I prayed silently, "Lord, You need to show up in a big way. I've been telling everyone all week that You will set people free from evil spirits, and now this young woman is manifesting in front of everyone." Then, taking a stand of faith in God's Word, I knelt on that floor, put my hand on her, and spoke, "In the name of Jesus Christ, I command this evil spirit to let her go now. Be free, in Jesus's name!" At that moment, the demon convulsed her and came out of her. She sat up in her right mind, and, through my interpreter, I asked her if she wanted to receive Jesus Christ as her Lord and Savior. "Yes," she answered, and I led her to the Lord in front of everyone. After prayer, the young woman stood up, set free, in her right mind, and completely saved. And the entire crowd, who had never heard of Jesus a few days earlier, began cheering and praising God for setting this young woman free!

From that night on, the crowds grew in number, and hundreds of people from this small village received Jesus as their Lord and Savior because of this young woman's deliverance. At the end of the crusade, we planted the very first church in that village, and the believers there are going strong to this day. This is exactly what the Word of God tells us should be a part of our life in Jesus. We should "preach everywhere, the Lord working with us and confirming the word through the accompanying signs." (See Mark 16:20.)

AN UBER DRIVER WHO NEEDS JESUS

Too many western Christians think that evil spirits are only present in faraway lands and third-world countries. However, that is not the case at all. Satan has his minions working all over this world. But, remember: *"Greater is he that is in you, than he that is in the world"* (1 John 4:4 KJV).

After a week of traveling for the ministry, Amanda and I flew into Orlando, Florida, and landed at the airport at around ten thirty at night. We arranged for an Uber driver to pick us up at the airport and drive us home. Our driver was a young Hispanic woman about twenty years old. Once we were on the interstate, I asked this young woman what she knew about Jesus, which I normally do when I begin witnessing to someone about the Lord. As soon as I mentioned Jesus, she grabbed the steering wheel firmly, pulled herself toward it, and made some strange facial expressions without answering my question.

Immediately, I knew in my spirit that there was something demonic going on. As I've shared, I'm used to seeing manifestations of the enemy in our gospel crusades and even in some of our meetings in the U.S. But I had never seen it in an Uber traveling 70 miles an hour down the highway! After holding herself rigid for about a minute, the young woman pushed herself back into her seat and responded to my original question. "Well," she said slowly, "I am originally from Puerto Rico, but I've been in the U.S. for several years with my family. We don't go to church often, so I don't know much about Jesus."

I asked her a second question: "Can I tell you what *I* know about Jesus?" Instantly, she grabbed the steering wheel hard and, still driving 70 miles per hour, pulled the car to the side of the highway. Cars were whizzing past us as we came to an abrupt stop on the shoulder of the road. The young woman opened the driver's door without getting out and threw up on the pavement below. Maybe you'd say she just happened to get sick, but I knew this was connected to what the Holy Spirit was showing me. Amanda and I began praying fervently in the backseat for her freedom. Within seconds, she jumped out of the vehicle and into the ditch beside the car and started throwing up violently. It was startling, but I knew that Jesus was in control.

JESUS CALLS ALL OF US TO SHARE OUR FAITH WITH EVERYONE, EVERYWHERE, WHENEVER POSSIBLE.

I got out of the car, walked over to the young woman, and began to pray over her to be set free, in Jesus's name. After a few minutes of prayer, she returned to her right mind and asked me shakily, "What was that? What happened to me?" I began sharing the gospel with her and told her that what she had experienced was from the devil, but that Jesus wanted us to pray for her to be set free. "Do you want to receive Jesus as your Lord and Savior?" I asked, but she said she wasn't ready yet. Shaken by her experience, she asked me to drive the car to her house so her mother could drive us home. As I drove, we assured her again that she could call on the name of Jesus at any time, and He would save her and set her free. Once we arrived at her house, her mom drove us home, and we were able to share the gospel with her, as well. What a night!

Some people might think being a preacher is only for Sunday morning services, but Jesus calls all of us to share our faith with everyone, everywhere, whenever possible. I know I may never see that young woman again, but in faith I believe that God was drawing her to Himself and that she will receive His gift of salvation. God did not send her to us by accident, and the Word will not return to Him without accomplishing His purposes. *"So shall My word be that goes forth from My mouth; it shall not return to Me void, but it shall accomplish what I please, and it shall prosper in the thing for which I sent it"* (Isaiah 55:11).

The Bible is not just a book you read and forget about, because there is transforming power in the Word of God. By reading and listening to God's Word, you get to know Him in a deeper way and are enlightened by His truth. Sharing God's Word is essential, and we can do it with boldness because of the Holy Spirit who resides within us. *"It is written"*—there is power in those three compelling words from Jesus to defeat the enemy. God's Word supplies us with the answers to overcome every attack of the devil. We can stand in faith on His promise that if we *"submit to God...[and] resist the devil...**he will flee from you***" (James 4:7), in Jesus's name.

NINE

A KEY TO FAITH IS PERSPECTIVE

"Perspective is everything when you are experiencing
the challenges of life."[28]
—*Joni Eareckson Tada*

*"I have been crucified with Christ; it is no longer I who live, but
Christ lives in me; and the life which I now live in the flesh I live by
faith in the Son of God, who loved me and gave Himself for me."*
—Galatians 2:20

Several years ago, while in Pakistan, I was invited to preach at a local
church. When I met the pastor, a man named Paul, he gave me some
background information about his ministry and then told me how he

28. Brainy Quote.com, "Joni Eareckson Tada Quotes," https://www.brainyquote.com/
quotes/joni_eareckson_tada_526384.

had established his church in a challenging part of the city. Instead of planting the church in a Christian community where he might have felt safe and where it would have been easier to fill the seats with Christians, Pastor Paul chose to plant his church in a non-Christian community so he could share the gospel with his Muslim neighbors.

I asked him, "How often do you receive persecution for being a Christian and planting this church right here in the city?"

"Well, we experience small persecutions almost every day of the week," he told me.

"What does a 'small' persecution look like?" I wanted to know. "And how does it differ from a 'big' persecution?"

Pastor Paul smiled and answered, "Small persecution means no death threats, just people discriminating against us, gossiping about us, slandering us. Telling people not to do business with our congregants and raising the price of everything because we're Christians—and other small threats here and there."

My follow-up question was serious: "How often do you receive big persecution?"

He told me, "Every one to two years, we will have something big happen."

"What did that look like the last time you received some big persecution?" I asked.

"Well, Pastor Chris, we received a serious persecution just a couple of years ago when some religious radicals came to burn down our church because they didn't want us to be here. First, they went to some of my congregations' houses, and they burned their houses down to the ground for being Christians and for living in this community. After that, the mob ran towards our church building to burn it down, as well," he told me.

"What happened?" I asked.

Here is the amazing answer he shared with me: "All the people who live around our church are Muslims, and we have a great relationship with them. They love us, and they love our church very much. So, our Muslim neighbors stood up to the mob who wanted to burn the church, saying, 'You will not burn this church down. These are good people, and we want them here. You will not burn down this church!'"

"So, the people surrounding the church saved it from being burned down?" I asked him.

"Yes," he affirmed. "We were so happy that the church was spared, but still, many of my congregants had their houses burned down, and I felt awful for those people."

I couldn't help but think about that story. When I went to his church the next day and stood there during the worship service, his congregation was truly worshiping Jesus. I've never in my life experienced such passionate worship as when I enter any church in Pakistan. These worshipers realize they could lose more than their houses at any moment—they could lose their lives for worshiping Jesus, for following Him, for living a Christian life. I know that there are many people who are saved at our crusades and, soon after, face extreme persecution even from family members. All because of their love for Jesus.

Recently, we had an amazing conference for pastors and leaders in Islamabad, Pakistan. The pastors are so hungry for God's Word and for revival, even though they have one of the hardest jobs in the entire world—preaching and ministering in the seventh most persecuted country in the world for Christians. It's my joy and honor to go into this nation to encourage and pour God's Word into them. I pray for these pastors daily, and I would love for you to do the same. They are champions for Jesus.

CHANGING YOUR LIFE'S PERSPECTIVE

Obviously, a Christian's life perspective in Pakistan is much different from our perspective in the U.S. and in other Western countries. Even though discrimination against Christians is growing here, we never face persecution like our brothers and sisters in the Middle East or in Asia, where Christians are being beaten, losing their homes, their livelihood, or their lives. Sadly, for many Christians in our part of the world, persecution means somebody failing to greet us with a smile when we walk into church. We often equate offense with persecution. I know this isn't true of every Christian in America, but our understanding and our perspective still needs to change radically for us to see the reality in so many other countries.

People often ask me, "Why would you go to a place where you could lose your life?" I had to face this question when I first decided to preach the gospel in countries that are unreached and dangerous. My heart burned to go to these places for Jesus, but even my perspective needed some adjustment. Our perspectives can change as we grow in our faith. Remember what I wrote earlier of the paralyzing fear that I felt on my first crusade when the guard was dancing and waving his gun on the rooftop? After speaking words of faith out loud from God's Word, that fear left and has never returned after eight years and twenty-five trips to Pakistan so far. God has been faithful to keep me and to remind me that He has called me there for a purpose. His Word declares that I will live and not die and that I will declare the works of the Lord. (See Psalm 118:17.)

PEOPLE OFTEN ASK ME, "WHY WOULD YOU GO TO A PLACE WHERE YOU COULD LOSE YOUR LIFE?"

I can proclaim with absolute confidence, "Jesus, I love You so much. You are my God, and I'm willing to do anything for You." I know without a shadow of a doubt that Jesus Christ is the Son of God, the Savior of the world. I'm willing to do whatever it takes to spread the gospel for Jesus.

As I shared earlier, since meeting Jesus, my heart has been on fire to go to the most difficult places in the world, places where people don't want to go, to bring the gospel to those who have never heard of Jesus. Jesus died for those people just like He died for you and me. Jesus even died for His own enemies! It is my joy and passion to go into these unreached towns and villages to bring the good news of Jesus Christ to the lost. Jesus surrendered His life for you and me, not just so we could go to heaven, although that is His greatest gift to us. He also died for us so that we can live for Him, live the life that Christ has for us today—living for Jesus Christ on this earth. Leonard Ravenhill, a British evangelist in the twentieth century, often said, "This life is just a dressing room for eternity—that's all it is!"[29] So, my life perspective is that Jesus died for me, and so I am willing to go where He sends me and to face the same reality as the Christians in Pakistan and other persecuted countries. *"I have been crucified with Christ; it is no longer I who live, but Christ lives in me; and the life which I now live in the flesh I live by faith in the Son of God, who loved me and gave Himself for me"* (Galatians 2:20).

---

29. Ark Haven Ministries, "The Purpose of Life Is Preparing for Eternity," https://arkhaven. org/now-is-the-time-to-prepare/spiritual-preparation/lifes-purpose/.

THE WRONG POINT OF VIEW

Since perspective is everything, if you don't have the right perspective, you will see things from the wrong point of view. When you lose perspective, everything is skewed. There was a time when I worked as a land surveyor, and we had to calibrate our machines to be able to put in perfectly straight lines for roads or buildings. If our machines were off just half a degree at the base, it could mean that the building or road would be off by several feet a few hundred meters down the line. One little degree off at the very start can cause you to be off by miles when you go a long distance. And so, perspective is everything.

Consider the two perspectives of Joseph while betrothed to Mary, the mother of Jesus. First, he finds out she is pregnant with a child that is not his. To make things even worse, she tells him the child's father is not another man from their village, but that God Himself caused her to become pregnant. Then suddenly, Joseph's perspective changes from not believing Mary and even wanting to "put her away secretly" to God's perspective. Matthew 1:20 tells us that an angel of the Lord appeared to Joseph in a dream and told him not to be afraid of taking Mary as his wife, *"for that which is conceived in her is of the Holy Spirit. And she will bring forth a Son, and you shall call His name Jesus, for He will save His people from their sins"* (Matthew 1:20–21). Wow! What a whirlwind of emotions Joseph must have experienced. His first perspective is to quietly rid himself of Mary and the child. However, once he knows God's plan, his entire perspective changes. Joseph realizes it is God's will for his life.

OUR PERSPECTIVE IN EVERY SITUATION MUST BE FROM HEAVEN'S PERSPECTIVE, NOT OUR OWN.

When you know God's will, it ultimately changes your perspective. Remember, God's Word is God's will for our lives. Our perspective in every situation must be from heaven's perspective, not our own. What does heaven's perspective look like? How does God see our situation? Notice that when Joseph was afraid of the situation, it was not heaven's perspective. A good rule of thumb is that if you're afraid of something, it's probably not God's perspective, because God does not give us a spirit of fear, nor is He the author of fear.

When you have the world's perspective, you protect your life by doing everything that the world tells you is right. I'm not necessarily saying that is always wrong, but our focus should not be on what we can physically do to protect ourselves but on what God has already done to protect us. Jesus has already paid the price for us to be healed. God has already promised protection for those who follow Him. Psalm 91 is a great example of God's protection for us during a war, or even a plague, such as the Covid-19 pandemic, which created so much fear across the world. The Bible tells us in Psalm 91 that no evil will befall you and no plague (or pandemic) will come near your dwelling. *"Because you have made the* LORD, *who is my refuge, even the Most High, your dwelling place, no evil shall befall you, nor shall any plague come near your dwelling"* (Psalm 91:9–10).

If we don't have God's perspective, we will have the world's perspective that causes us to live in paralyzing fear. One of the main problems that I see in the world today is that the media is putting out all this fear and propaganda. Since the media is run by people who don't necessarily follow Jesus, they put a worldly perspective into everything they broadcast or write. What we as believers need is to have the Lord's perspective. So, what is God's perspective? God's perspective is: "Even though I die, yet shall I live." (See John 11:25–26.)

HAVE FAITH IN GOD'S PROTECTION

God will protect us because His Word declares that no evil will befall us, and no plague will come near my dwelling. Psalm 91 also says that though a thousand fall at my side, and 10,000 at my right hand, it will not come near me. (See Psalm 91:7.) Isaiah 41:10 declares, *"Fear not, for I am with you; be not dismayed, for I am your God. I will strengthen you. I will help you and uphold you with My righteous hand."* The Bible tells us that God will protect us, that He is our shield, fortress, and strong tower. He is our deliverer, and no weapon formed against us will prosper or succeed. (See Isaiah 54:17.) Heaven's perspective is that God will protect us; therefore, we can walk in faith even while dying to ourselves and living out our life for Jesus.

While the the world's perspective tells us to do everything we can to save our lives, the Lord is sharing His perspective of the upside-down kingdom. We don't find salvation by saving ourselves. We find salvation by losing ourselves and giving ourselves completely to the Lord. We see the heavenly perspective in Luke 9:24-26, one of my favorite passages. Jesus is preparing His disciples to have God's perspective before He transfers His ministry to them.

In Luke 9:24–26, Jesus declares:

For whoever desires to save his life will lose it, but whoever loses his life for My sake will save it. For what profit is it to a man if he gains the whole world and is himself destroyed or lost? For whoever is ashamed of Me and My words, of him, the Son of Man will be ashamed when He comes in His glory, and in His Father's, and of the holy angels.

WE FIND SALVATION BY LOSING OURSELVES AND
GIVING OURSELVES COMPLETELY TO THE LORD.

So, what is Jesus saying? Jesus is saying that if you want to follow Him, you must be willing to have the perspective that comes from losing your life for Him. That doesn't mean you'll lose your life physically, but you must have a mentality to do whatever Jesus asks of you. Clearly, Jesus was preparing His disciples for the prospect that one day they might lose their life for Him. In the end, all the original apostles, with the exception of John, and many of Jesus's other followers were martyred for the gospel. As Christians, we must live with an *eternal* perspective and remember that what we do in this life will affect how we spend eternity. As followers of Jesus, we know that our life is eternal. With this perspective, we will actively imitate the life and teaching of Jesus Christ.

The disciples sat at the feet of Jesus, listening to the Master's teaching. Undoubtedly, they knew that Jesus Christ was the Son of God, the Messiah, and they were willing to give their lives for Him. Following Jesus's death and resurrection, the apostles spread the gospel, and the church grew quickly, but so did their persecution. That is why we should have the same perspective that Jesus provided to His disciples. What's the perspective I am referring to? *"Then Jesus said to His disciples, 'If anyone desires to come after Me, let him deny himself, and take up his cross, and follow Me. For whoever desires to save his life will lose it, but whoever loses his life for My sake will find it'"* (Matthew 16:24–25). Lay your life down along with the cares of this life. Don't try so hard to save this life; don't do anything out of fear, chaos, and worry about protecting this life. Rather, trust God with everything, even your very life.

GOD'S PROTECTION IN DANGER

Just a couple of years ago, we received an invitation to do a crusade in one of the most dangerous places to preach the gospel in Pakistan. For safety reasons, I will not share that town's actual name or location, but let's call it *Extreme-astan*. Extreme-astan is known around the country as one of the training grounds for radical extremists. The city is in a very rural area where there aren't many good jobs or opportunities, and, as a result, terrorist organizations go there to recruit people who are desperate for money or financial stability.

Extreme-astan has at least seven known training camps surrounding the city where radicals are trained. Each camp is like a compound with a Mosque in the center and training rooms surrounding it where they train people for Jihad. After their training is complete, the militants are sent throughout Pakistan, into Afghanistan or anywhere in the Middle East, to cause chaos and death. After seeking the Lord's direction, we agreed that this would be a great place to do a gospel crusade! When in that region of Pakistan, we usually stay in a modern hotel in Lahore that has strong security and safe food for our Western stomachs. However, since Extreme-astan is about six hours from Lahore, we decided to get a hotel that was three hours closer to our destination.

The week of the crusade, we arrived in Pakistan on a Tuesday and discovered that the Pakistani government had just arrested the newly elected president of one of the main extremist groups for spreading hate speech including slogans of "death to Pakistan's prime minister." It might sound crazy, but these things are somewhat normal in Pakistan, so it didn't faze me. Our crusade was scheduled to take place on Friday night, and I was confident that God would protect us. Our gospel campaigns in Pakistan are only one night; the government won't allow us to do multiple nights in a row due to potential retaliation from radicals.

Since we were going to a dangerous region for the crusade, we decided to hire more security guards. We also planned to do a small ceremony on Friday night and invite some of the Muslim leaders from Extreme-astan to come to sit with us on the stage so that we could bless them publicly for coming. We hoped that if some of them participated, they would be friendlier and wouldn't attack our crowd. In reality, it was still a very dangerous campaign to pull off. We needed heaven's perspective that God was for us and that we could trust Him with our lives; *"If God is for us, who can be against us?"* (Romans 8:31).

> WE NEEDED HEAVEN'S PERSPECTIVE THAT GOD WAS FOR US AND THAT WE COULD TRUST HIM WITH OUR LIVES.

The day of the crusade arrived, and as we waited for our security team to come to our hotel, we heard men shouting, horns honking, and cars rumbling on the street below. It was a major traffic jam moving toward the city of Lahore. I asked my team what was going on, and they informed me, "There are major riots today in Lahore. The entire city is on lockdown. No one can get in or out of the city, and even the internet and phones are shut off!" I thought, "Whoa! Thank You, Lord! If we had stayed in a hotel in Lahore, we never would have gotten out to do the crusade in time."

"Why is Lahore having riots today?" I asked.

I was informed, "All of the extremists in Pakistan are in Lahore to protest the arrest of their newly elected president, and they chose to do the protest today. They are burning cars in the streets and have even killed a few police officers already."

I was shocked, and I asked, "You mean to tell me that all the extremists chose today to leave their training camps and compounds in Extreme-astan to go to Lahore and protest? The very day we are having our crusade?"

"Yes, that's right, brother!"

And we praised God for His faithful plan to protect us!

While they were in Lahore protesting, we gathered our security team and went in the opposite direction to Extreme-astan and did our crusade in total peace. As a result, 50,128 people received Jesus Christ as their Lord and Savior that night. Hallelujah!

My friends, we can trust God with our lives. When you know what God has called you to do, when you know His Word and have His perspective, you can rest assured that you're in God's will and that He will protect you. Heaven's perspective is everything. When you know what God's Word says, you know what heaven's perspective is, and you can conquer any obstacle the enemy might throw your way.

LIVE FOR JESUS

As you read these words, say them out loud with faith: "Jesus, You are my source of life. My life is only given to me because You gave it. Not because I protect it, not because I keep it, but because You are the author of life and have given me the very breath in my lungs."

I WANT TO ENCOURAGE YOU TODAY TO GIVE YOUR ALL TO JESUS.

When you have this perspective, it is easier to say, "Jesus, I'll do whatever You want me to do. I'll go wherever You want me to go. I'll say whatever You want me to say. And I don't care if people judge me; I don't care if people persecute me. Jesus, I love You so much. Even if it costs me my life to share Your love with people worldwide, I'll freely give it because I know when I pass from this life into the next, I will be with You. My life is not finished here." Our lives are not our own. We have been bought with a price—the precious blood of Jesus. The old things have passed away, all things are new—that establishes a heavenly perspective for us. Your new life will produce new life in others. Die to yourself and live for Jesus.

I want to encourage you today because you might not have that perspective. Maybe you don't know Jesus in that way as a friend, but today you can know Him. You can have a relationship with Him and receive His forgiveness of sin. The Bible says that He will fill you with His Spirit, and faith will rise up within you because your life was bought by Him. He died to set you free, and then He rose from the dead. Never forget: because He rose, because He is alive, you and I will also live, even though we die. I want to encourage you today to give your all to Jesus. Live your whole life for Him!

TEN

EXPANDING THE KINGDOM OF GOD

"No Christian is in a right condition if he is not seeking
in some way to bring souls to Christ."
—C.H. Mackintosh

*"And this gospel of the kingdom will be preached in all the world as
a witness to all the nations, and then the end will come...."*
—Matthew 24:14

The kingdom of heaven and the kingdom of God are two phrases in the New Testament that Jesus used interchangeably. In Matthew 19:23 Jesus says that it would be hard for a rich man to enter the kingdom of heaven, adding, *"It is easier for a camel to go through the eye of a needle than for a rich man to enter the kingdom of God."* You see Jesus's parallel use of the kingdom of heaven and the kingdom of God show these phrases to be synonymous. Once you see this, it changes everything. Jesus isn't just referring to a heavenly kingdom where we will go to spend eternity. He's talking about a spiritual reality that is available for us to enter right here and now.

The Jews were anticipating a *physical* kingdom, not a *spiritual* kingdom. However, while standing before Pilate at His trial, Jesus said, *"My kingdom is not of this world"* (John 18:36). This certainly reinforces the *spiritual* nature of His kingdom. The kingdom of God is a spiritual reality that transcends the kingdoms of this world. Jesus told His disciples that the kingdom of heaven is *at hand*. (See Matthew 4:17.) Jesus's first coming is the kingdom's inauguration, meaning that Jesus is the immediate, present experience of the kingdom of heaven. Jesus said the kingdom is here with us now. (See Matthew 12:28.) In Luke 17:21, He said that *"the kingdom is within you."* A better translation would be that the kingdom of God is in your midst. Once I understood that the kingdom of God is here and now, it changed everything. At that point as a young Christian, I realized that the kingdom of God and the kingdom of Satan are at war in the heavenlies and on the earth. As Christians, we must actively participate in taking territory from the kingdom of hell and advancing the kingdom of God on this earth.

I HAVE ONE AMBITION IN LIFE

I have one ambition in life, that the world might know Him—Jesus Christ, the Savior of the world. *"And this gospel of the kingdom will be preached in all the world as a witness to all the nations, and then the end will come…"* (Matthew 24:14). Our mission statement can be summed up like this: *We have one vision, one mission…the Great Commission.*

God is raising up people across the earth, filling them with His Spirit, and sending them out to "turn the world upside down" as the early disciples did. *"These men who have turned the world upside down have come here too"* (Acts 17:6). God wants to raise up His sons and daughters today to receive the same power and to go out in Jesus's name to shake up the world! It's not about being special. On the day of Pentecost, the room of 120 was filled with ordinary people—fishermen, a tax collector, women whose sins had been forgiven by Jesus. I believe in these last days God is raising up everyday people like you and me and filling us with the Holy Spirit so that we can turn the world upside down for Jesus.

GOD IS RAISING UP PEOPLE ACROSS THE EARTH, FILLING THEM WITH HIS SPIRIT, AND SENDING THEM OUT.

"Lord, if You can use Peter and John, the people in my church, my pastor or that evangelist, then I know You can use me." I never thought God would take me, an ordinary man from a dairy farm in central Minnesota, and send me around the world to preach the gospel to millions of people. It's not by my power! It's by the power and will of almighty God. There is power in *supernatural faith without limits* where the impossible happens, where we can see mountains cast into the sea in Jesus's name. (See Mark 11:22–23.) There is power in the baptism of the Holy Spirit where God fills you to overflowing and enables you to do things you never could have done before. Our ministry could never have been orchestrated by me in the natural. It is only by the Holy Spirit's leading and power that salvations and miracles are happening. Jesus invites us to a partnership with Him, so that His kingdom will advance, and nothing will stop it.

My friends, for the kingdom's sake, we must continue to push forward until we reap the harvest! Our God is a big deal, for He is awesome and powerful, and He has said:

I am the LORD, and there is no other; there is no God, besides Me. I will gird you, though you have not known Me, that they may know from the rising of the sun to its setting that there is none besides Me. I am the LORD, and there is no other. I form the light and create darkness, I make peace and create calamity; I, the LORD, do all these things. (Isaiah 45:5–7)

EVANGELISM IS WARFARE

Evangelism is a type of offensive warfare in which we engage to liberate captives from Satan's territory and transfer them to Christ's kingdom. Gospel preaching, church planting, and discipleship are offensive warfare against the kingdom of darkness. Offensive warfare aims to restore, liberate, and establish God's kingdom on earth today. All we need to do is lay hold of God's Word, preach the gospel, heal the sick, and cast out demons when necessary, to make disciples. Hell's gates will not stop you from advancing God's kingdom. The kingdom of hell will not stop you from living a victorious life.

Even now, the kingdom of God is advancing in some of the most persecuted countries on the planet, including China, Iran, Pakistan, Afghanistan, and Saudi Arabia. Most Christians don't understand this truth, as stated in the book of Acts, that some time the kingdom is advanced through persecution. *"On that day a great persecution broke out against the church in Jerusalem, and all except the apostles were scattered throughout Judea and Samaria. Godly men buried Stephen and mourned deeply for him"* (Acts 8:1–2 NIV). Those who were scattered went everywhere preaching the Word. The kingdom was advancing in a culture of persecution, and the church was expanding. They thought people would flee and hide, but it was the opposite. *"Blessed are those who are persecuted because of righteousness, for theirs is the kingdom of heaven"* (Matthew 5:10 NIV). In His faithfulness, God raises up people *in* these persecuted nations, and He raises up people *to go* to these persecuted nations to preach the gospel and advance His kingdom.

> OFFENSIVE WARFARE AIMS TO RESTORE, LIBERATE, AND ESTABLISH GOD'S KINGDOM ON EARTH TODAY.

Many people think that the greatest enemy of the church is the advancement of Islam, or the corruption of a communist dictator persecuting the church, or even warlords in various countries creating issues for Christians there. But, my friends, the greatest enemy of the church is lukewarm Christianity. God is looking to raise up people who will be on fire for Him! Who will unashamedly preach the gospel of salvation through the power of the Holy Spirit and set the captives free around the world in the mighty name of Jesus!

Our greatest enemies cannot be fought and defeated in the physical realm. I am grateful for our military, and for our veterans; every country needs a military to protect it and give it security. But the only way we are going to destroy the evil that exists in this world is to advance the kingdom of God. Evil lies within the heart, and there is only one person who can change peoples' hearts—His name is Jesus Christ! Remember, when we preach the gospel, the people who receive Jesus literally go from darkness to light, from the power of darkness to the power of light, and from the kingdom of hell to the kingdom of heaven—and this is how we advance the kingdom of God. That's why evangelist Reinhard Bonnke often said that he wanted to "plunder hell to populate heaven."

THE GREAT COMMISSION

Amanda and I just returned from the Everyone Conference in Amsterdam led by Empowered21 and the Global Evangelist Alliance (GEA). The focus, of course, was evangelism and a GEA Initiative to mobilize and evangelize the world for Jesus Christ in the next 10 years—by 2033, which is the 2,000-year anniversary of the church at Pentecost. There are eight billion people living in our world today, and we want every one of them to have the opportunity to hear the message of Jesus Christ.

Jesus clearly commissioned us to go out into the world. His last statement to His followers before He left the earth was a command. It was the most important thing He wanted them to remember, don't you think? Jesus spoke to them, saying,

> *"All authority has been given to Me in heaven and on earth. Go therefore and make disciples of all the nations, baptizing them in the name of the Father and of the Son and of the Holy Spirit, teaching them to observe all things that I have commanded you; and lo, I am with you always, even to the end of the age."* (Matthew 28:18–20)

There are many things we can do to honor Jesus, but this is the *one thing* that He wanted to leave as His parting words on earth. Jesus assures His followers that He will be with them to help complete their work until the end of the age. And then He will return. As the disciples stood gazing up at Jesus as He ascended, two angels spoke to them, *"Men of Galilee, why do you stand gazing up into heaven? This same Jesus, who was taken up from you into heaven, will so come in like manner as you saw Him go into heaven"* (Acts 1:11). While we are waiting for Jesus to return, His last command still stands, *"Go into all the world and make disciples."* That's our call, to fulfill the last thing He commanded until He returns.

In the Great Commission, Jesus was speaking to His followers. That means that if you are a believer, a follower of the Lord Jesus Christ, He is speaking to you. *"Go therefore and make disciples of all the nations."* Not some, not just your nation or mine; all the nations! You know, Jesus knew this wouldn't be possible without the Holy Spirit who was sent to empower us, lead us, and guide us into all truth.

Even though Jesus's intent was clear, many Christians are not involved in any way with spreading His message. My friends, there are eight billion people on the planet, and billions of them have yet to hear the gospel. Jesus has commanded every follower to go into all the world with His message and make disciples of all people. So, how are we going to steward this command? What are we going to do with it? *"And this gospel of the kingdom will be preached in all the world as a witness to all the nations, and then the end will come..."* (Matthew 24:14). We are on this planet for one reason: to reach people for Jesus Christ. He wants to see one more soul saved, and then one more after that, and then one more after that...before He returns at the end of the age.

WE ARE ON THIS PLANET FOR ONE REASON: TO REACH PEOPLE FOR JESUS CHRIST.

FIVE KEYS TO REACHING THE WORLD FOR CHRIST

God calls each of us to take our place in the battle for souls. Maybe you would say, "But I have not been called to be an evangelist! I can't speak easily about my faith." Even if being an evangelist is not your calling, there is a place for you in this mission. I want to share five keys with you for reaching the entire world for Jesus Christ.

Number One: *Train the church to be Spirit-empowered witnesses for Jesus.*

God wants the church to be empowered by the Holy Spirit so that we can be dynamic witnesses for Jesus. The Great Commission is not just for evangelists! In the book of Acts, in addition to the apostles, we see believers who are still about the Father's business. That can be you! Christians often refer to these as "laypeople" because they don't hold a specific title that relates to ministry, but you have the power to share the gospel of Jesus Christ with your families, friends, coworkers, and even strangers at the grocery store. In the early church, the New Testament wasn't even written yet. The gospel was spread in power by word of mouth. Thousands of Christians were confessing that Jesus had died and risen again to pay for their sins and to give them eternal life with Him. Confessing your faith in Jesus Christ out loud is a sure way to advance the kingdom of God.

"*And* [Jesus] *Himself gave some to be apostles, some prophets, some evangelists, and some pastors and teachers, for the equipping of the saints for the work of ministry, for the edifying of the body of Christ*" (Ephesians 4:11–12). Jesus Christ has called some in the body of Christ to serve in one of the fivefold offices in the church—"*apostles, prophets, evangelists, pastors, and teachers*"—and they are called to equip the saints for "*the work of ministry.*"

Those called to the office of evangelist can equip the rest of the body to help—all of us working together to bring the gospel message of Christ to the whole earth. "*For we are His workmanship, created in Christ Jesus for good works, which God prepared beforehand that we should walk in them*" (Ephesians 2:10). I can't do it alone! None of us can do it alone. Not even the greatest evangelists of the twentieth century, such as Billy Graham or Reinhard Bonnke, could do it alone.

Go out and share the gospel with those in your sphere and beyond. Your church may have an evangelism team or a missions council; learn how to share your faith from their teaching and example. Find ways to support those who go out into the world with the message of Jesus, with your time, your prayers, and with your possessions, so that the gospel will continue to be spread throughout the world in Jesus's name.

Number Two: *Train young crusade evangelists to go out in the world.*

The good news of Jesus Christ must be proclaimed out loud. It can't be the gospel unless it is preached. Remember Paul's word to the Romans on this point: *"How then shall they call on Him in whom they have not believed? And how shall they believe in Him of whom they have not heard? And how shall they hear **without a preacher**?"* (Romans 10:14). Evangelists who are called to go out to other nations around the world need to be supported and trained.

As I have shared, Amanda and I were trained at Christ For the Nations Institute and also through the mentoring of evangelists Daniel Kolenda and Reinhard Bonnke. One ministry that offers evangelism training is Christ For All Nations Bootcamp; another is Global Evangelism Alliance, an online association for evangelists. In addition, we conduct training through our ministry, Chris Mikkelson Evangelistic Ministries. Many denominations have evangelism programs as well, such as the Assemblies of God and others that specialize in preparing evangelists for the work of the kingdom. Perhaps God is calling you to receive this training or to support others through your prayers and/or fiannces as they train to reach the world for Christ.

Number Three: *Use social media and online teaching platforms.*

When Jesus commanded His followers to go out into all the world to preach the gospel, He knew about future inventions that would enable us to do exactly that! From the black-and-white televised gospel crusades of Billy Graham to the high-powered satellite connections across the world today, these tools have been used to spread God's Word to millions. Did you know that, today, 79 percent of the world's population above the age of eighteen is using some form of social media?! Detailed analysis by the team at Kepios (an organization that tracks digital use around the world) confirmed that there were 4.95 *billion* social media users around the world in November 2023, which is 61.4 percent of the total global population. "However, comparing social media users with figures for total population may under-represent the full extent of social media use, because most social media companies restrict use of their platforms to people aged 13 and above. The latest data suggests that the number of "adult" social media users around the world (i.e. over the age of 18) now equates to almost 79 percent of all the adults in that age group."[30] That is an astronomical number!

> MINISTRIES THROUGHOUT THE WORLD USE THE INTERNET TO COMMUNICATE THE POWER OF THE GOSPEL FOR JESUS.

The internet offers many different platforms for sharing the gospel truth. Reach out to your friends and acquaintances through social media by sharing your faith and by posting Spirit-filled messages of faith and truth from evangelists and preachers that you follow. You likely have people in your friends lists who have never heard the gospel before. Through platforms like YouTube, Instagram, and Facebook, among others, you can post teaching and preaching videos sharing the message of Jesus—easily reaching people near and far with the message of salvation.

30. Datareportal, "Global Social Media Statistics," https://datareportal.com/social-media-users.

Even though Satan means to use the internet for evil, God, who is so much greater, is using it for good to expand His kingdom! Ministries throughout the world use the internet to communicate the power of the gospel for Jesus. Over the last eight years, through the Holy Spirit, the number of people worldwide who watch our online messages has exploded. Hundreds of thousands around the world follow us on social media, YouTube, and our website to hear the gospel of salvation and to be prayed for to receive healing in Jesus's name! By God's grace, our weekly TV show, *Salvation Today*, airs in 73 countries across the globe. If you multiply our outreach alone by all the other Christian ministries and Christ followers who use the internet, we can go to the ends of the earth with the salvation message of Jesus! I am humbled by the opportunity God has given us to reach the lost for His Son Jesus.

Number Four: Collaborate.

Evangelistic ministries around the world can collaborate, thereby multiplying their efforts to reach all the countries on earth. *How beautiful upon the mountains are the feet of him who brings good news, who proclaims peace, who brings glad tidings of good things, who proclaims salvation, who says to Zion, "Your God reigns!"* (Isaiah 52:7)

As evangelistic teams have come together to focus on one country at a time for Jesus, I have been invited to preach in parts of the world I have never visited before. In recent weeks, we have received invitations to preach in Ethiopia, South Africa, Egypt, El Salvador, Australia, and Kenya. I have also been invited to return to Pakistan and India to proclaim the good news that *our God reigns!* Today, there are evangelists from around the world joining efforts to bring the masses to Jesus Christ. As the body of Christ, we are more powerful and productive when we work together than when we are apart. As we move out to reach the world for Jesus, these joint efforts will be duplicated by teams of disciples around the world. Just as Jesus commanded nearly 2,000 years ago!

*WE ARE MORE POWERFUL AND PRODUCTIVE
WHEN WE WORK TOGETHER THAN
WHEN WE ARE APART.*

Number Five: *Send.*

*"How shall they preach **unless they are sent?**"* (Romans 10:15). Perhaps you are still thinking, "I could never do what you are doing. I know I'm not called to be an evangelist." Then what is God asking of you to help fulfill the Great Commission? Again, is it giving of your time, your prayers, your substance?

> *Now it came to pass, afterward, that He [Jesus] went through every city and village, preaching and bringing the glad tidings of the kingdom of God. And the twelve were with Him, and certain women who had been healed of evil spirits and infirmities—Mary called Magdalene, out of whom had come seven demons, and Joanna the wife of Chuza, Herod's steward, and Susanna, and many others who provided for Him from their substance.* (Luke 8:1–3)

If we are honest, we can see that Jesus couldn't do ministry without support. The Bible tells us in Luke 8:3 that many people provided for Jesus so that He could minister for the Father. What can you do? You could be one of those who provides for evangelism with your substance. There are people in your church, your city, or your country who need support for their ministry to the world. It says in Deuteronomy 32:30 that one can chase a thousand but two can put ten thousand to flight. If we work together for God's kingdom, much more can be accomplished than if we work alone.

THE ONLY THING WE CAN TAKE TO HEAVEN IS OTHER PEOPLE WHO HEARD THE GOSPEL BECAUSE OF OUR OBEDIENCE.

Only the message of salvation through Jesus Christ can save the world. Politics cannot save the world. Politics are not eternal, but the Word of God is. Only what is done for eternity will last. And the only thing we can take to heaven is other people who heard the gospel because of our obedience. It takes radical generosity to send evangelists throughout the nations for Jesus. God loves a cheerful giver; and as a result, He will *"bless you abundantly, so that in all things at all times, having all that you need, **you will abound in every good work**"* (2 Corinthians 9:8 NIV). God blesses us materially and spiritually so that we will have an abundance for every good work, which means finding your territory to take for the kingdom of God.

Life is a compilation of moments where you say yes. Let every yes be for the glory of God! Let's work together in faith to expand the kingdom of God throughout all the earth until Jesus Christ returns!

"AND THESE SIGNS WILL FOLLOW"

And He said to them, "Go into all the world and preach the gospel to every creature. He who believes and is baptized will be saved; but he who does not believe will be condemned. And these signs will follow those who believe: in My name they will cast out demons; they will speak with new tongues; they will take up serpents; and if they drink anything deadly, it will by no means hurt them; they will lay hands on the sick, and they will recover." (Mark 16:15–18)

As we reach the world with the gospel of Christ, the Lord uses signs and wonders to confirm His Word. That is why we rejoice when the Spirit moves at our crusades; it's because of the word of faith that people are saved, healed, and delivered. It confirms our words that Jesus Christ is still alive on this earth and that He welcomes them into His kingdom.

My friend, the Bible tells us in the book of Mark that these signs (demons being cast out, people speaking with tongues, the sick being healed) will follow them that believe. Are you a believer? Then you qualify to perform miracles. Are you filled with the precious Holy Spirit? Then you have the anointing and power of the Holy Spirit within you to perform miracles. The only thing left is just believing that God wants to use you to see souls saved and people healed. You can activate miracles by faith in the Word of God and by the power of the Spirit.

In this book, I have shared some of the supernatural events that I have seen personally in my life and ministry. We serve a supernatural God, and I desire that these accounts inspire you to trust him, wholeheartedly serve Him, and live a supernatural lifestyle. Since being saved in 2006, I have seen the Lord perform countless miracles. Thousands of people have experienced healing in our crusades. We've seen hundreds of people set free from evil spirits, and countless signs and wonders have happened that all bring glory and honor to God. Today, the supernatural is a normal part of my life. The supernatural life is the normal life you and I are meant to see as born-again believers in Christ.

Maybe you're saying, "Chris, I'm just an elementary school teacher, or a firefighter, or a laborer; I'm not a professional preacher." But Jesus didn't say that these signs will follow professional preachers; He didn't say these signs will follow only pastors or evangelists; He said these signs will follow *them that believe.* That's you! If you believe in Jesus Christ as Lord and Savior, you qualify to preach the gospel and heal the sick. You qualify for *activating miracles.* The only way we can enter into the supernatural is by believing. It's by radical faith in a supernatural God. When we put our faith in Him, anything is possible.

The greatest miracles usually take place sometime between saying amen and then waiting to see what happens. When you pray, pray in faith and expect the miraculous. Often, before praying for someone who is sick, I ask them how bad the pain is on a scale of 1-10 before I pray for them. Then, I ask them after I pray if the pain has subsided to a lower number. In this way, I know that God is moving, and I stand in faith to see the pain reduced all the way to zero in Jesus's name!

"AND THEY WILL RECOVER"

Are you afraid to step out in faith? When I first began to evangelize in public, Amanda and I would go to train stations with friends and preach the gospel to people waiting for their boarding time. We had a captive audience! We would take a fold-up step stool with us everywhere we went and would stand on top of it to preach. One day, we were at the train station in Houston, and I was standing on the stepstool sharing the gospel with a dozen people when a young boy walked up behind me. He was leaning on crutches, and his foot was in a brace due to a serious injury from an accident.

GOD IS LOOKING FOR PEOPLE LIKE YOU WHO WILL ADVANCE HIS KINGDOM WITH THE GOSPEL OF JESUS CHRIST.

While I continued preaching, Amanda and our friends began to pray for the young boy to be healed. As they prayed, the power of God touched him, and the pain began to subside. As a test, he started walking without the crutches to see if the pain was completely gone. Shouts of joy rose up behind me, and I turned to see the crutches lifted in the air and the young boy beaming from ear to ear! His bright smile testified that he had been completely healed. I turned around and shouted to the crowd, "This boy has been healed! God has healed him by the prayer for the sick today. God did this in your sight to let you know that He is real! Turn to Jesus today; give your life to Him! He is real. He can heal, and He can save you." I made a call for salvation, and two people in that crowd received Jesus Christ as their Lord and Savior, in part because of seeing the power of God heal a young boy that day. Stepping out in faith was the way we learned to activate miracles. It is the way you can learn as well.

My friend, God isn't looking for "professional Christians." God is looking for people like you who will advance His kingdom with the gospel of Jesus Christ. He's looking for Christians who will believe in His miracle-working power, who will have supernatural faith without limits to stand on His Word, who will preach the gospel of Jesus Christ with His anointing, and who will lay hands on the sick to see them recover.

As a Christian, you qualify to see the lost saved; you qualify to receive the anointing power of God; you qualify to activate miracles in Jesus's name. Pray in faith, trust God's Word, stand on the power of the Holy Spirit, and watch what God will do through your life. Promise me this—that you will always give Jesus Christ all the glory and all the praise when you see those salvations and miracles come to pass in His name. Without Him we can do nothing! It's all about Jesus—giving Him the glory, seeing His name lifted high above all others, and seeing the world come to the saving knowledge of Jesus Christ.

Now go, therefore, and preach the gospel, introduce Jesus to a hurting world, and walk in supernatural faith. *"Freely you have received, freely give"* (Matthew 10:8) to everyone you encounter! God bless you.

ABOUT THE AUTHOR

Chris Mikkelson is an international evangelist whose passion is to see souls saved, the sick healed, the church equipped to preach the gospel with demonstrations of the Spirit and power, and worldwide revival. Chris preaches the gospel in some of the most remote, unreached, and dangerous nations of the world, primarily near the Middle East, where the number of Christians is 2 percent or less. Multitudes have attended his large gospel campaigns, where he has preached to several million people, and hundreds of thousands have been saved and baptized in the Holy Spirit. To date, Chris has led over two million people to Jesus Christ, mostly in the nation of Pakistan. His campaigns are marked by healings and deliverances, confirming the preaching of the gospel, according to Mark 16. He has seen people's blind eyes and deaf ears opened, those who were paralyzed walk, incurable diseases reversed, and countless miracles to God's glory.

Chris and his wife, Amanda, who also has a passion for souls and is highly involved in the ministry, are graduates of Christ For The Nations Institute (CFNI) in Dallas, Texas. After graduation, Chris served under the ministry of evangelists Daniel Kolenda and Reinhard Bonnke, first as a personal assistant to Kolenda and then as Bonnke's USA crusade director, before launching his own international ministry in 2015. His passion to see God moving in our midst has made him a sought-after speaker at churches, conferences, and revival services worldwide. His *Salvation Today* television program is broadcast to millions of households worldwide and is also available on Facebook and YouTube. For more information, please visit chrismikkelson.com. Chris and Amanda currently reside in Orlando, FL, the headquarters of Chris Mikkelson Evangelistic Ministries.

Welcome to Our House!

We Have a Special Gift for You

It is our privilege and pleasure to share in your love of Christian books. We are committed to bringing you authors and books that feed, challenge, and enrich your faith.

To show our appreciation, we invite you to sign up to receive a specially selected **Reader Appreciation Gift**, with our compliments. Just go to the Web address at the bottom of this page.

God bless you as you seek a deeper walk with Him!

WE HAVE A GIFT FOR YOU. VISIT:

whpub.me/nonfictionthx

WHITAKER
HOUSE